Multiple Choice Questions in Library & Information Science

MULTIPLE CHOICE QUESTIONS
in
Library & Information Science

Shehbaz Husain Naqvi
Lecturer, BLIS Course

Dr Zakir Husain Library
Jamia Millia Islamia
New Delhi-110025

Ess Ess Publications

4837/24, Ansari Road, Darya Ganj,
New Delhi-110002
☎ : 23260807, 41563444
Fax : 011-41563334
E-mail: info@essessreference.com
url:http://www.essessreference.com

First Published 2009

Published by SUMIT SETHI
for Ess Ess Publications
4837/24, Ansari Road, Darya Ganj,
New Delhi - 110 002
Ph. : 23260807, 41563444
Fax : 011-41563334
E-mail: info@essessreference.com
url:http://www.essessreference.com

ISBN : 978-81-7000-571-1

Price : Rs. 175/-

Laser Typesetting:
Mukesh Graphics
T-1264, Mangolpuri, New Delhi
Ph. : 9899079035, 20106135
E-mail:mukeshgraphics29@yahoo.com

Printed at :
Print Line

Contents

Preface

MCQs in Library & Information Science offer a complete new approach to the different areas of Library & Information Science Education.

It is in fact a humble attempt to bring MCQs in a nutshell to the knowledge of students of Library & Information Science.

The book is divided into nine chapters. Seven chapters deal with specific branch of Library & Information Science. One chapter deals with true and false and other with fill in the blanks.

A number of Textbooks, Periodicals and Reference Books related to Library & Information Science were consulted in compiling the MCQs in the field of Library & Information Science.

My thanks to my beloved parents, sisters and colleagues who have inspired me in this endeavor and also my gratitude to M/s ESS ESS Publishers, New Delhi who have brought out this publication with utmost care.

We would heartily welcome suggestions, comments, and criticism if any from readers for the improvement of the work.

Shehbaz Husain Naqvi

Syllabus of UGC-NET Library and Information Science (Code No.: 59)

Note: There will be two question papers. Paper-II will cover 50 Multiple Choice Questions (Multiple choice, Matching type, True/False, Assertion-Reasoning type) carrying 100 marks and Paper-III will have two Parts-A and B. Part-A will have 10 short essay type question (300 words) carrying 16 marks each. There will be one question from each unit with internal choice from the same unit. Total marks will be 160. Part-B will be compulsory and Questions will be set from Unit-I to Unit-X. The candidate will attempt one question from Part-B (800 words) carrying 40 marks. Total marks of Paper-III will be 200.

PAPER-II and PAPR-III (Part A & B)

Unit-I

Information, Information Science, Information Society

Information as a Resource/Commodity

Information Transfer Cycle-Generation, Collection, Storage and Dissemination, Role of information in Planning, Management, Socio-economic Development, and Technology transfer.

Communiation – Channels, barriers

Intellectual Property Rights – Concept, Copyright, Censorship – Print and Non-print Media.

Library and Information Policy at the National Level.

Unit-II

Laws of Library Science

Library Resource Sharing and Networking

Library Movement and Library Legislation in India

Library Extension Services

Library and Information Science Education in India

Library and Information Profession

Library Associations in India, UK and USA-ILA, IASLIC, IATLIS, SIS, LA, ASLIB, SLA and ALA.

Library Associations/Organisations at International level – FID, IFLA and UNESCO.

Unit-III

Sources of Information – Primary, Secondary and Tertiary – Documentary and Non-documentary.

Reference Sources – Encyclopedias, Dictionaries Geographical Sources, Biographical Sources, Year-books/Almanacs, Directories, and Handbooks, Statistical (salient features and evaluation).

Bibliographical Sources-Bibliographies, Union Catalogues, Indexing and Abstracting Journals (salient features and evaluation).

E-documents, E-books, E-Journals.

Databases-Bibliographic, Numeric and Full text-Evaluation.

Unit-IV

Reference and Information services, Referral Service

Bibliographic Service, Indexing and Abstracting Service, CAS, SDI, Digest Service, Trend Report.

Online Services

Translation Services

Reprographic Services

Unit-V

Organisation of knowledge/information

Modes of formation of subjects

Library Classification-Canons and Principles

Library Classification Schemes –DDC, UDC and CC

Library Cataloguing-Canons and Principles

Library Cataloguing Codes-CCC and AACR-II

Bibliographic Records-International standards-ISBDs, MARC and CCF

Indexing-Pre-coordinate, Post-coordinate

Vocabulary Control-Thesaurus, Lists of Subject Headings

Databases-Search Strategies, Boolean Operators

Knowledge Management.

Unit-VI

Management-Principles, Functions, Schools of Thought

Planning, Organisation Structure

Decision making

System Study-Analysis, Evaluation and Design

Collection Development-Books, Serials, Non-book Materials-Selection

Acquisition, Maintenance; ISBN, ISSN, Cataloguing-in-Publication (CIP)

Human Resources Management-Manpower

Planning, Job analysis, Job description, Selection, Recruitment, Motivation Training and Development, Staff Manual, Leadership and Performance Evaluation.

Delegation of authority

Financial Management-Resource Generation, Types of Budgeting, Cost and Cost-Benefit analysis.

PERT, CPM

Library Buildings and Equipments

Performance Evaluation of Libraries/Information Centres and Services

Marketing Information product and services

Total Quality Management (TQM).

Unit-VII

Information Technology-Components; Impact of IT on Society

Computers – Hardware, Software, Storage-Devices, Input/Output Devices Telecommunication-Transmission media. Switching systems, Bandwidth, Multiplexing, Modulation, Protocols, Wireless Communication.

Fax, E-Mail, Tele-conferencing/Video-conferencing, Bulletin Board Service, Teletext, Videotex, Voice Mall.

Networking-Concepts, Topologies, Type-LAN, MAN and WAN

Hypertext, Hypermedia, Multimedia

Integrated Services Digital Network (ISDN), Open Systems Interconnection (OSI).

Unit-VIII

Library Automation – Areas of automation, Planning, Hardware and Software Selection, OPAC.

Networks-ERNET, NICNET, DELNT, JANET, BLAISE, OCLC, INFLIBNET

INTERNET-Components, Services, Browsing-Web Browsers, Search Engines Meta-Data, Digital Object Identifier (DOI).

National and International Information Systems – NISSAT, NASSDOC, INSDOC,DESIDOC,INIS, AGRIS, MEDLARS, INSPEC.

Unit-IX

Types of Research – Basic, Applied, Interdisciplinary

Research Design

Scientific Method, Hypotheses, Data Collection, Sampling

Methods of Research-Historical, Descriptive, Case Study, Survey, Comparative and Experimental

Statistical Methods, Data Analysis

Report Writing

Research Methods in Library and Information Science and Services

Bibliometrics

Unit-X

Types of Libraries-National, Public, Academic and Special-Objectives, Structure and Functions.

Digital Libraries-Concept

Virtual Libraries-Concept

Types of users, User studies, User education

Role of UGC in the growth and development of libraries and information centers in institutions of higher education in India.

Role of Raja Ram Mohan Roy Library Foundation (RRLF).

Unit-I

Information, Communication & Society

1. ISR stands for:
   (i) Information Sources Retrieval
   (ii) Indexing, sorting and Retrieval
   (iii) Indexing system of research methods
   (iv) Information storage and retrieval

2. First Copyright Act in India was enacted in :
   (i) 1954 (ii) 1914
   (iii) 1957 (iv) 1916

3. Which one of the following technical committee was set up for standardization work in documentation field.
   (i) ISA-46 (ii) ISA-33
   (iii) ISA-39 (iv) ISA-40

4. ANSI headquarters is located at :
   (i) Chicago (ii) New Jersey
   (iii) New York (iv) Washington, DC

5. "Information Science" is more popular in:
   (i) Germany (ii) Russia
   (iii) U.K. (iv) U.S.A.

6. The term "Informatics" is used in France for:
   (i) Information Retrieval
   (ii) Indexing System

(iii) Machine processing of data

(iv) Manually retrieval of information

7. "Informatologia Yugoslavica" is name of a:
   (i) A periodical
   (ii) An Institute
   (iii) A documentation centre
   (iv) A society

8. The terms "Information Retrieval: was first used by:
   (i) F.W. Lancaster (ii) Wynhdham Hulme
   (iii) Calvin Mooers (iv) Paul Otlet

9. Indian Patent Office is located at:
   (i) Kolkatta (ii) New Delhi
   (iii) Pune (iv) Nagpur

10. "INFOTERM Series" is published by:
    (i) INFLIBNET, Ahmedaba
    (ii) INFONET, New Delhi
    (iii) IASLIC, Kolkatta
    (iv) INFOTERM, Paris

11. ICIREPAT is an international organizations associated with:
    (i) Information Retrievals
    (ii) Standards
    (iii) Patents
    (iv) Information Exchange

12. "Knowledge is a sum total of information conserved by civilization", is a definition of knowledge given by:

(i) Dr. S.R. Ranganathan

(ii) J.S. shera

(iii) Machlup

(iv) Lancaster

13. Which one of the following is not an approach to information?

(i) Current approach

(ii) Everyday approach

(iii) Catching-up approach

(iv) Leisure approach

14. Main three types of information requirements were given by:

(i) Mikhailov
(ii) Melvin Voigt
(iii) Vickery
(iv) S.C. Bradford

15. Which one of the following information need requires almost all relevant information documents to users?

(i) Exhaustive approach

(ii) Everyday approach

(iii) Brusting-up approach

(iv) Current approach

16. In which of the information approach, the need of information is continuous one?

(i) Exhaustive approach

(ii) Current approach

(iii) Catching-up approach

(iv) Everyday approach

17. Which one of the following services is provided on demand of the user?

(i) Journal Circulation (ii) Newspaper Clipping
(iii) SDI (iv) CAS

18. When communication takes place without bringing the lien of Authority in consideration,. it is called?
    (i) Informal Communication
    (ii) One-way communication
    (iii) It is not a communication process
    (iv) Diagonal communication

19. The origin of 'Library'is from:
    (i) Ltin word Liber
    (ii) Greek word Libra
    (iii) English word Librar
    (iv) None of these

20. Which one of the information gathering technique uses direct contact with user?
    (i) Interview method
    (ii) Questionnaire method
    (iii) Diary method
    (iv) Observation by self

21. Which one of the following is related to development of team "informatics"?
    (i) Calvin Mooers
    (ii) Mikhailov
    (iii) Paul Otlet
    (iv) Henri La Fontaine

22. IPR stands for:
    (i) International Patent Registration.
    (ii) Information Processing & Retrieval

(iii) Intellectual Property Rights

(iv) Internet Protocol Rights

23. Shanon-Weaver Model is studied in :

(i) Cataloguing practices

(ii) Classification schedules

(iii) User Education

(iv) Information & Communication

24. ISO is associated with:

(i) Information storage

(ii) Information Standardization

(iii) Intellectual system organization

(iv) Standardization Agency

25. According to Matchlup, the difference between Information and knowledge is:

(i) Information increases with use, whereas knowledge is constant

(ii) Information is stimulatory, whereas knowledge is practical

(iii) Information is shareable, whereas knowledge is one's property

(iv) Information is piecemeal, fragmented, particular, whereas knowledge is structured, coherent and universal.

26. New name of "American Documentation Institute is:

(i) American Documentation Centre

(ii) United States Centre of Documentation.

(iii) American Information Resource Centre

(iv) Knowledge & Learning Centre

27. An instrument which is defined as "Government grant of exclusive privilege of making/selling the new inventions" is known as:
(i) Power of Attorney (ii) Specifications
(iii) Patents (iv) Standards

28. The term Information Science was coined in:
(i) 1955 (ii) 1959
(iii) 1961 (iv) 1963

29. The term Informatics was coined in USSR in:
(i) 1962 (ii) 1964
(iii) 1966 (iv) 1968

30. The term Informatics was used in place of:
(i) Library Science
(ii) Information Science
(iii) Reference Service
(iv) Documentation

31. The credit for coining the term Information goes to:
(i) S.R.Ranganathan
(ii) Calvin Mooers
(iii) H.P. Luhn
(iv) Chernyi and Gilyarevarki

32. Biggest consumers of information are:
(i) Students (ii) Researchers
(iii) Teachers (iv) All the above

33. Who suggested that 'One big library is the basic factor for bibliographical control:
(i) Weston Davis (ii) D.J. Foskett
(iii) J.D. Bernal (iv) Alvin Wiegnberg

34. Who suggested to impose bibliographical control one big journal is sufficient"
    (i) J.D. Bernla
    (ii) S.R.Ranganathan
    (iii) Western Devis
    (iv) Alvin Weignberg

35. Who coined the term 'Information Retrieval':
    (i) S.R. Ranganathan
    (ii) Calvin Mooers
    (iii) F.W.Lancaster
    (iv) Alfred J. Lotka

36. The term Information Retrieval was used in the year:
    (i) 1940 (ii) 1945
    (iii) 1950 (iv) 1955

37. The term 'Recall' is used in information retrieval to refer to the ability of a system to :
    (i) Withhold irrelevant documents
    (ii) Respond to a query without loss of time
    (iii) Retrieve relevant documents
    (iv) Recall a specific document

38. The basic difference between SDI and other modes of Current Awareness is that SDI is:
    (i) Directed to wards the needs of an individual user/project
    (ii) A computer based information service
    (iii) Provided only at the local level
    (iv) Provided only to the top managers

39. What is routing of journals:
    (i) Reference service
    (ii) Information service
    (iii) Current Awareness Service
    (iv) Selective Dissemination of Information

40. Among the following which is not a NISSAT Sectoral Center:
    (i) National Chemical Laboratory
    (ii) National Informatics Center
    (iii) Central Drug Research Institute
    (iv) ATIRA

41. World Science Information System refers to
    (i) UNISIST (ii) NATIS
    (iii) DEVSIS (iv) ISDS

42. The first director of DRTC was:
    (i) P.N. Kaula (ii) S.R.Ranganathan
    (iii) A.Neelameghan (iv) B.S. Kesavan

43. 'Universal Bibliographic Control' is a call given by:
    (i) UNESCO (ii) IFLA
    (iii) UNO (iv) ICSU

44. Which of the following is not the feature of an information retrieval system:
    (i) Relevance (ii) Recall
    (iii) Precision (iv) Perception

45. In which of the following types of indexes are access points not derives automatically:
    (i) KWIC (ii) Citation Indexing
    (iii) KWOC (iv) POPSI

46. DELNET is a:
    (i) Wide area network (ii) Local area network
    (iii) National network (iv) Regional network

47. RLIN stands for:
    (i) Regional Library and Information Network
    (ii) Research Library Information Network
    (iii) Regional Library for Information
    (iv) Research Library and Integrated Network

48. Which one is the barrier for information communication :
    (i) Classification (ii) Censorship
    (iii) Indexing (iv) Weeding out

49. Intellectual Property Rights are recognised as:
    (i) Copyright (ii) Patent
    (iii) Neither (i) or (ii) (iv) Both (i) and (ii)

50. Size to size reproduction of documents is called:
    (i) Reduction (ii) Enlargement
    (iii) Fascimile (iv) None of the above

51. Growth of information beyond manageable limit is known as :
    (i) Information growth
    (ii) Information dynamics
    (iii) Exponential growth
    (iv) Information explosion

52. The concept of 'Technological Gatekeepers' was first proposed by:
    (i) Allen (ii) Diana Crane
    (iii) Solla Price (iv) B. Guha

53. Which of the following is a Union Catalogue:
    (i) Ulrich's Periodical Directory
    (ii) New Serials Titles
    (iii) Press in India
    (iv) NUCSSI

54. What is the function of Referral Centre:
    (i) Which directly gives information
    (ii) Which provides information directly to the enquirer
    (iii) Which does not provide information directly to the enquirer.
    (iv) Which does not provide information directly to the enquirer but suggest sources.

55. Notification of new arrivals in the library is a :
    (i) SDI service
    (ii) CAS service
    (iii) Reference service
    (iv) Information service

56. The feedback mechanism is the most important component of:
    (i) Translation service
    (ii) Reprography service
    (iii) CAS service
    (iv) SDI service

57. The direct method of electrostatic photocopying is known as:
    (i) Zerography
    (ii) Electrography
    (iii) Thermography
    (iv) Electrofax

58. Free indexing language is commonly used in :
    (i) Citation indexes
    (ii) Computer-based system
    (iii) Pre-coordinate indexing system
    (iv) Post-coordinate indexing system

59. ASLIB Cranfield Research Project was mainly concerned with:
    (i) Classification and cataloguing
    (ii) Information retrieval
    (iii) Evaluation of indexing system
    (iv) Selective Dissemination of Information

60. 'GISTRNIC' is a part of :
    (i) SIRNET
    (ii) INFLIBNET
    (iii) DELNET
    (iv) NICNET

Answer Sheet

1. (iv)	2. (ii)	3. (i)	4. (iii)
5. (iv)	6. (iii)	7. (i)	8. (iii)
9. (iv)	10. (iv)	11. (iii)	12. (i)
13. (iv)	14. (ii)	15. (i)	16. (ii)
17. (iii)	18. (iii)	19. (i)	20. (i)
21. (ii)	22. (iii)	23. (iv)	24. (iv)
25. (iv)	26. (i)	27. (iii)	28. (ii)
29. (iii)	30. (ii)	31. (iv)	32. (ii)

33. (i)	34. (i)	35. (ii)	36. (iii)
37. (iii)	38. (i)	39. (iii)	40. (ii)
41. (i)	42. (ii)	43. (ii)	44. (iv)
45. (iv)	46. (iv)	47. (iv)	48. (ii)
49. (iv)	50. (iii)	51. (iv)	52. (i)
53. (iv)	54. (iv)	55. (ii)	56. (iv)
57. (iv)	58. (ii)	59. (iii)	60. (iv)

Unit – II

Library and Society

1. Headquarters of IFLA is situated at :
   (i) London (ii) Hague
   (iii) Paris (iv) New York

2. UBC stands for :
   (i) United Books Corporation
   (ii) Universal Bibliographic Code
   (iii) Universal Bibliographic Control
   (iv) Universal Bibliographic Classification

3. ASLIB is library association of :
   (i) UK (ii) USA
   (iii) Australia (iv) Spain

4. CILIP is a Library Association of:
   (i) United Kingdom
   (ii) United States of America
   (iii) Spain
   (iv) Canada

5. "Traite de Documentation" was published by:
   (i) Henri La Fontaine (ii) Paul Otlet
   (iii) F.W. Lancaster (iv) C.A. Cutter

6. The term GILA is a associated with:
   (i) Indexing system
   (ii) Information Storage System

(iii) Directory of Govt. of India Libraries
(iv) None of these

7. Which of the following library is state central library of Tamil Nadu State?
(i) Khuda Baksh Oriental Public Library
(ii) Connemara Public Library
(iii) Asiatic Society Library
(iv) Central Reference Library

8. Name of ruler of Baroda, who is associated with Public Library Movement there:
(i) Maharaja Sayaji Rao Gaekward-III
(ii) Maharaja Ranjit Singh
(iii) Maharaja Todar Mal
(iv) Maharaja Gulab Singh

9. In which year Ranganathan joined as a librarian in BHU?
(i) 1946 (ii) 1947
(iii) 1943 (iv) 1945

10. Paul Otelt & Henry La Fontaine were from:
(i) America (ii) Britain
(iii) Chinese (iv) None of the above

11. Classification Research Group is located at :
(i) New Delhi (ii) Chicago
(iii) London (iv) Paris

12. A library is also known as :
(i) Store house (ii) Cultural centre
(iii) Information centre (iv) None of the above

13. Which one is channel of communication:
    (i) One-way channel
    (ii) Private Party Channel
    (iii) Formal channel
    (iv) Government Channel

14. Which open of the following is National Input centre for UNESCO's Index Translatonium?
    (i) National Science Library
    (ii) National Library
    (iii) Parliament Library
    (iv) Defence Science Library

15. During vedic period, knowledge was divided into one of the following branches:
    (i) Moksha (ii) Poesy
    (iii) Logic (iv) Concrete

16. K (S) + a = K (S+ S) is an equation related to:
    (i) Bibliometric Laws
    (ii) Definition of vocabulary control
    (iii) Definition of knowledge
    (iv) Information Retrieval Techniques

17. Kothari Education Commission was setup in:
    (i) 1958 (ii) 1967
    (iii) 1964 (iv) 1966

18. Indian Gandhi National Centre for Arts (IGNCA) was established in :
    (i) 1981 (ii) 1945
    (iii) 1986 (iv) 1976

19. ISO recommendation for transliberation is :

(i) ISO/R9-1955 (ii) ISO/R4-1953
(iii) ISO/TC-46 (iv) ISO/DR-1278

20. ISO recommendation for abbreviation of periodical titles is:
(i) ISO/R690-1968 (ii) ISO/TC-46
(iii) ISO/DR-1278 (iv) ISO/R4-1953

21. Which of the following persons are related to FID?
(i) Henry La Fontaine and Paul Otlet
(ii) Michael Gorman and Paul Winkler
(iii) S.R. Ranganathan and G. Bhattacharya
(iv) Henri Fayol and F.W. Taylor

22. Which one of the following library is not of national importance?
(i) National Library of India
(ii) Delhi Public Library
(iii) Saraswati Mahal Library
(iv) Central Reference Library

23. Name of Imperial Library (Calcutta) was charged to National Library (Calcutta) by the Act of :
(i) 1984 (ii) 1903
(iii) 1948 (iv) 1956

24. In which law of library science, Ranganathan uses the concept of growth and development?
(i) Fifth Law (ii) Fourth Law
(iii) First Law (iv) None of the above

25. Five Laws of library science were first conceived in _____ and published in:
(i) 1927; 1929 (ii) 1923; 1925

(iii) 1945; 1948 (iv) 1930; 1931

26. Which one of the following is communication system of Russia.
    (i) INTELSAT (ii) AGRIS
    (iii) DEVSIS (iv) INTERSPUTNIK

27. Which one of the following is intermediary between information user and its generation?
    (i) Reprographic System
    (ii) Information System
    (iii) Indexing System
    (iv) Abstracting System

28. Which one of the following Indian state first passed the Library Legislation?
    (i) Jammu & Kashmir
    (ii) Uttaranchal
    (iii) Tamil Nadu
    (iv) Andhra Pradesh

29. ALA was established in :
    (i) 1907 (ii) 1845
    (iii) 1857 (iv) 1876

30. Which is the third law of library science?
    (i) Every book its reader
    (ii) Every reader his/her book
    (iii) Save the Time of reader
    (iv) Books are for use.

31. ISO recommendation for bibliographical references is ?
    (i) ISO/R690-1968 (ii) ISO/DR-1278
    (iii) ISO/TC-46 (iv) ISO/R4-1953

32. Which one of the following is not a characteristic of knowledge?
    (i) It is infinite (ii) It is fragmented
    (iii) It is dynamic (iv) It is coherent

33. DRTC is located at:
    (i) Kolkatta (ii) Pune
    (iii) Mumbai (iv) Bangalore

34. The full name of S.R. Ranganathan is:
    (i) Shri aman Ranganathan
    (ii) Shiyali Ramanrita Ranganathan
    (iii) Shiv Ranano Ranganathan
    (iv) None of the above

35. What is the correct sequence of the following according to their decrease in coverage?
    (i) Law – Principle– Cannon
    (ii) Canon – Law – Principle
    (iii) Law – Canon – Principle
    (iv) Law – Canon – Principle – Hypothesis

36. In the name of S.R.Ranganathan, "Shiyali" is the name of :
    (i) His wife
    (ii) His mother
    (iii) His Elder Sister
    (iv) His Village

37. In which year 49th FID conference was held:
    (i) 1998 at Delhi (ii) 1996 at Jaipur
    (iii) 1989 at Shimla (iv) 1981 at Delhi

38. Year 1930 is an important landmark is Indian Librarianship because:
    (i) National Public Library Act was passed
    (ii) Dr.S.R. Ranganathan was awarded 'Bharat Ratna"
    (iii) ILA was established
    (iv) None of these

39. The Advisory Committee for libraries was appointed in :
    (i) 1964 (ii) 1957
    (iii) 1948 (iv) 1975

40. Which one of the following is depository library, under D.B Act of 1954?
    (i) Rampur Raza Library
    (ii) Central Secretariat Library
    (iii) British Council Library
    (iv) Delhi Public Library

41. Which of the following associations are associated with teachers of library science in India.
    (i) IASLIC (ii) IATLIS
    (iii) ASLIB (iv) GILA

42. Which one of the "Five Laws of Library Science" makes it obligatory for state to provide state library authority?
    (i) First Law (ii) Fourth Law
    (iii) Second Law (iv) Fifth Law

43. "Bibliotheque Nationale-de-Paris" is located at :
    (i) London (ii) Paris
    (iii) Toronto (iv) Chicago

44. Who was fist Chairman of UGC?
    (i) Dr. C.D. Deshmukh
    (ii) Dr.S.R.Ranganathan
    (iii) Dr. Kothari
    (iv) Dr.Manmohan Singh

45. Standardisation bodies are mainly concerned with three topics, which of the following is one of it?
    (i) Abstracting
    (ii) Transliteration
    (iii) Translation
    (iv) None of the above

46. Mass Media is a kind of communication Channel:
    (i) Formal Channel
    (ii) AR Entertainment media
    (iii) Two-way channel
    (iv) Informal Channel

47. Any process where there is "an exchange and exact replication of thoughts, feelings, facts, belies and ideas between and among the individuals" is known as:
    (i) Communication Process
    (ii) Information Retrieval Techniques
    (iii) Vocabulary control techniques
    (iv) Knowledge conservation techniques

48. Which one of the following is not essential element of communication system.
    (i) Communication
    (ii) Message
    (iii) Interpreter
    (iv) Recipient

49. Which one of the following is barrier to communication?

(i) Lack of interest

(ii) Lack of need

(iii) Lack of understanding of foreign language documents

(iv) None of the above

50. The term "Informatics" is generally used in :

(i) USA (ii) France

(iii) Russia (iv) Germany

51. Indian Library Association (ILA) was established at :

(i) Bangalore (ii) New Delhi

(iii) Pune (iv) Kolkatta

52. Library Day is celebrated in :

(i) 14th February (ii) 14th July

(iii) 20th December (iv) 5th September

53. Madras Library Association was formed in :

(i) 1972 (ii) 1982

(iii) 1925 (iv) 1928

54. Ranganathan get an idea about analytico-synthetic classification scheme by seeing:

(i) Library of Congress (ii) British Museum

(iii) BHU Library (iv) Meceano set

55. Which one of the following is an international body:

(i) IFLA (ii) ALA

(iii) ILA (iv) DRTC

56. ILSA is an

(i) Indexing journal

(ii) Dept. of Library & Information Science Journal

(iii) Current Information Source
(iv) Abstracting journal

57. Connemara Library is a State Central Library of :
(i) Tamil Nadu (ii) Kerala
(iii) Goa (iv) Miroran

58 Library cess is a source of income for:
(i) School Library
(ii) Private Library
(iii) Public Library
(iv) University Library

59 DELNET stands for:
(i) Delhi Library Network
(ii) Developing Library Network
(iii) Digital Library Network
(iv) None of the above

60 Andrew Carnegie belongs to :
(i) UK (ii) Russia
(iii) Ukrain (iv) USA

61. Who is known as Ranganathan of Pakistan:
(i) Mazid Ali Khan (ii) Mohd K Ahmad
(iii) Dr Hameed (iv) Dr Khursheed

62 Who was teacher of Dr Ranganathan in London:
(i) Anthony Pannizi (ii) W.C.B Sayers
(iii) H.E.Bliss (iv) J.D.Brown

63 Ranganathan started designing Colon Classification in:
(i) 1919 (ii) 1872
(iii) 1924 (iv) 1914

64. The definition of public library is given in:
    (i) Indian Constitution
    (ii) IASLIC constitution
    (iii) ILA constitution
    (iv) UNESCO Public Library Manifesto

65. Library of Congress is located at :
    (i) New York (ii) New Jersey
    (iii) Washington, DC (iv) Toranto

66. Delhi Public Library was inaugurated on:
    (i) 27th October 1951 (ii) 15th August 1951
    (iii) 1st April 1951 (iv) 14th August 1951

67. National Archieves of India are located at :
    (i) Kolkata (ii) New Delhi
    (iii) Bangalore (iv) Pune

68. Central Secretariat Library (CSL) is managed by :
    (i) Ministry of Information & Broadcasting
    (ii) Ministry of Human Resource Development
    (iii) Cabinet Secretariat
    (iv) Ministry of Culture

69. Which one of the following falls under Oriental Libraries?
    (i) Rampur Raza Library
    (ii) National Library
    (iii) Asiatic Society Library
    (iv) British Council Library

70. Which one of the following is chairperson of university Library Committee?
    (i) Librarian (ii) Registrar

(iii) Vice-Chancellor (iv) None of the above

71. Special Library is maintained through:
(i) Govt. Grant (ii) Public fund
(iii) Library Cess (iv) None of the above

72. "Library of Congress" (USA) is equivalent to:
(i) Parliament Library of India
(ii) National Science Library of India
(iii) National Archieves of India
(iv) Central secretariat Library of India

73. W.A. Border was associated with Public Library Movement in:
(i) Madras (ii) Birmingham
(iii) Baroda (iv) Yorkshire

74. Kenyon Committee was set up for Library development in:
(i) UK (ii) Kenya
(iii) Paris (iv) Nigeria

75. What is date of birth of Dr. S.R. Ranganathan?
(i) 14 August 1901 (ii) 16 August 1901
(iii) 25 August 1901 (iv) 15 August 1901

76. Which one of the following is special feature of Public Libraries?
(i) Literature Search (ii) Extension Service
(iii) Abstracting Service (iv) CAS

77. Raja Ram Mohan Roy Library Foundation is working for :
(i) Creating awareness abut Ranganathan
(ii) Betterment of Academic Librarianship

(iii) Development of Public Libraries
(iv) None of the above

78. Library of ISRO (India) comes under the category of :
(i) Academic Library
(ii) Full-Automated Library
(iii) Defence Library
(iv) Special Library

79. The first true Public Libraries Act of UK was passed in :
(i) 1849 (ii) 1850
(iii) 1854 (iv) 1852

80. Asiatic Society Library is located at
(i) Mumbai (ii) Kolkatta
(iii) Chennai (iv) New Delhi

81. There is no separate Department of Public libraries in :
(i) Andhra Pradesh (ii) Uttar Pradesh
(iii) Tamil Nadu (iv) Karnataka

82. CDRI is located at :
(i) Lucknow (ii) Haridwar
(iii) Pune (iv) New Delhi

83 . National Institute of Oceanography is located at :
(i) Chennai (ii) Hyderabad
(iii) Goa (iv) Mumbai

84. UNESCO's Manifests on Public Libraries was first formulated in:
(i) 1948 (ii) 1949

(iii) 1972 (iv) 1994

85. The first mobile library was started in :
    (i) Karnataka (ii) Kerala
    (iii) Haryana (iv) Tamil Nadu

86. The term 'Library Science' was first used by:
    (i) J. Mills
    (ii) W.C. Berwick Sayers
    (iii) Melvil Dewey
    (iv) S.R.Ranganathan

87. Ranganathan was appointed as National Research Professor in Library Science by government of India in:
    (i) 1965 (ii) 1966
    (iii) 1967 (iv) 1968

88. The concept of 'Librametry' was developed by:
    (i) A.W. Gouldner (ii) S.R. Ranganathan
    (iii) M. Murphy (iv) G.R. Lyle

89. Name given by S.R. Ranganathan for Book Mobiles is
    (i) Janitor (ii) Mobile van
    (iii) Library on Wheels (iv) Librachine

90. Which honour was awarded to Dr. Ranganathan by Government of India in recognition of his services in the field of Library Science and Librarianship:
    (i) Rao Sahib (ii) D.Litt.
    (iii) Padmashri (iv) Padma Bhushan

91. The first Indian book on Library Science entitled 'Primer of Librarianship' was written by:
(i) S.R. Ranganathan (ii) D.N. Marshall
(iii) Asa Don Dickenson (iv) None of the above

92. Who has authored 'Putting Knowledge to Work'.
(i) Jesse H. Shera (ii) S.R. Ranganathan
(iii) A.J. Wells (iv) Pauline Atherton

93. Who coined the term 'Paperless society':
(i) S.R. Ranganathan (ii) F.W. Lancaster
(iii) Calvin Mooers (iv) None of the above

94. Who remarked 'Some books are to be tested, others are to be swallowed, and some few to be chewed and digested...
(i) Melvil Dewey (ii) William Shakespeare
(iii) S.R. Ranganathan (iv) Francis Bacon

95. To resolve the conflict between two Canons, an appeal can be made to:
(i) Postulates (ii) Principles
(iii) The Five Laws (iv) None of the above

96. In which of the Five Laws of Library Science, library legislation is emphasized:
(i) First Law (ii) Second Law
(iii) Third Law (iv) Fourth Law

97. Which of the following is associated with 'Child growth' and 'Adult growth':
(i) Second Law (ii) Third Law
(iii) First Law (iv) Fifth Law

98. Books for all is a variant of:

(i) First law i.e. Books are for use.
(ii) Second law i.e. Every reader his/her book
(iii) Third law, i.e. Every book its reader
(iv) None of the above

99. The 'Open Access' to library shelves contributes to the fulfillment of:
(i) First law of library science
(ii) Second law of library science
(iii) Third law of library science
(iv) Fifth law of library science

100. The first Act of Parliament to provide free public library service was passed in Great Britain in the year:
(i) 1826 (ii) 1850
(iii) 1876 (iv) 1881

Answer Sheet

1. (ii)	2. (iii)	3. (i)	4. (i)
5. (ii)	6. (iii)	7. (ii)	8. (i)
9. (iv)	10. (iv)	11. (iii)	12. (iii)
13. (iii)	14. (ii)	15. (i)	16. (iii)
17. (iii)	18. (iii)	19. (i)	20. (iii)
21. (i)	22. (ii)	23. (iii)	24. (i)
25. (iv)	26. (iv)	27. (ii)	28. (iii)
29. (iv)	30. (i)	31. (i)	32. (ii)
33. (iv)	34. (ii)	35. (iii)	36. (iv)

37. (i)	38. (iii)	39. (ii)	40. (iv)
41. (ii)	42. (iii)	43. (ii)	44. (i)
45. (ii)	46. (i)	47. (i)	48. (iii)
49. (iii)	50. (iii)	51. (iv)	52. (iii)
53. (iv)	54. (iv)	55. (i)	56. (iv)
57. (i)	58. (iii)	59. (ii)	60. (iv)
61. (i)	62. (ii)	63. (ii)	64. (iv)
65. (iii)	66. (i)	67. (ii)	68. (iv)
69. (i)	70. (iii)	71. (iv)	72. (i)
73. (iii)	74. (i)	75. (i)	76. (ii)
77. (iii)	78. (iv)	79. (ii)	80. (i)
81. (iii)	82. (i)	83. (iii)	84. (ii)
85. (iv)	86. (iv)	87. (i)	88. (ii)
89. (iv)	90. (iii)	91. (iii)	92. (iv)
93. (ii)	94. (iv)	95. (iii)	96. (ii)
97. (iv)	98. (i)	99. (iii)	100. (ii)

Unit-III

Reference and Information Services

1. "New Encyclopdia Britannica" is published from:
   (i) Philadelphia (ii) New Jersey
   (iii) New York (iv) Chicago

2. "Keesing's Record of World Events" is a:
   (i) Current Information Source
   (ii) Secondary Information Source
   (iii) Informal Information Source
   (iv) A kind of grey literature.

3. "Grey Literature" means :
   (i) Computer peripherals
   (ii) Unpublished seminar reports
   (iii) Archival documents
   (iv) AV materials

4. "Asian Recorder" is published from:
   (i) New York (ii) New Jersey
   (iii) New Delhi (iv) New Jalpaigudi

5. The recent ethnic violence in Paris (2005) will not be extensive covered in :
   (i) Asian Recorder
   (ii) Europa world yearbook
   (iii) Kessing's Record of world events
   (iv) Facts on File

6. University of Illinois publishes:
   (i) Journal of Documentation
   (ii) Journal of Information Science
   (iii) Library Trends
   (iv) Library Quarterly

7. Pamphlet is a document of a few printed pages, usually less than:
   (i) 5 pages (ii) 10 pages
   (iii) 49 pages (iv) 60 pages

8. Name of the Prime Minister of Australia can be found in :
   (i) India A Reference Annual
   (ii) World of Learning
   (iii) International Who's who
   (iv) Universities Handbook

9. Trade Literature is a ______ source of information:
   (i) Primary (ii) Secondary
   (iii) Tertiary (iv) None of these

10. Which source will be required to get information about Mr. Bill Clinton?
    (i) Facts on File
    (ii) Dictionary of Biography, Kolkatta
    (iii) Dictionary of Biography, London
    (iv) Dictionary of American biography

11. An incident in Afghanistan will get more coverage in:
    (i) Facts on File
    (ii) Keesing's record of world events

(iii) Asian recorder

(iv) None of these

12. Encyclopedia Britannica is divided into :
    (i) Three sections (ii) Four Sections
    (iii) Five Sections (iv) One Sections

13. Which part of Encyclopedia consist of outline of knowledge?
    (i) Complete book (ii) Micropaedia
    (iii) Macropaedia (iv) Propaedia

14. Encyclopedia of Library & Information Science is published by:
    (i) R.R.Bowker
    (ii) Marcel Dekper
    (iii) Collier and MacMillion
    (iv) None of the above

15. Main aim for publishing Trade Bibliographies is :
    (i) To help users (ii) To do business
    (iii) To help library staff (iv) All of the above

16. The frequency of SCI is :
    (i) Monthly (ii) Quarterly
    (iii) Bimonthly (iv) Weekly

17. Science Citation Index consist of :
    (i) One index (ii) Two indexes
    (iii) Four indexes (iv) Three indexes

18. Meta-document is a term given by:
    (i) Denis Grogan (ii) C.W. Hanson
    (iii) S.R.Ranganathan (iv) Paul Otlet

19. According to Ranganathan, "PATENT" is a document classed under:
    (i) Tertiary document
    (ii) Neo-conventional document
    (iii) Non-conventional document
    (iv) Informal source of information

20. "Union Catalogue" is a kind of information source:
    (i) Primary source (ii) Secondary Source
    (iii) Tertiary Source (iv) Meta-document

21. Main source of information for a catalogues is:
    (i) Title page (ii) Verso of title page
    (iii) In the end of book (iv) On the flap

22. Library of Congress – Accession List – South Asia is published from:
    (i) New Delhi (ii) Calcutta
    (iii) Colombo (iv) New York

23. "Indian Books is Print" are published from:
    (i) New Delhi (ii) Kolkatta
    (iii) Pune (iv) Chennai

24. UNESCO's International book year was :
    (i) 1975 (ii) 1972
    (iii) 1927 (iv) 1957

25. The Editor of "Encyclopedia of Librarianship" is:
    (i) S.R. Ranganathan (ii) Melvil Dewey
    (iii) F.W. Lancaster (iv) Allen Kent

26. "Current Contents" is published by:
    (i) Institute of Scientific Information (Philadelphia)

(ii) Indian Institute of Science

(iii) University of Illinois

(iv) National Medial Library

27. Role Operator (2) is PRECIS stands for :

(i) Aggregate (ii) Target/Form

(iii) Part/Property (iv) Acton/Effect

28. Which one of the following canons was past to be propounded:

(i) Canon of Recall value

(ii) Canon of Permanence

(iii) Canon of context

(iv) Canon of currency

29. The "Guide to reference material" is published by:

(i) H.W. Wilson (ii) Forest Press

(iii) Walford (iv) R.R.Bowker

30. A Union Catalogue is :

(i) A catalogue of Trade Unions

(ii) A catalogue of Manuscripts

(iii) A catalogue of group of libraries

(iv) A catalogue of foreign language books

31. Which one of the following document will be read from first line to last line?

(i) Rogets Thesaurus

(ii) Encyclopedia of library & Information Science

(iii) Dictionary of Inorganic Chemistry

(iv) Textbook of Organic Chemistry

32. A basic difference between a library catalogue and a bibliography is:

(i) Library catalogue is in card form only.

(ii) Library catalogue can only be consulted I the library

(iii) Library catalogue is published by librarian only

(iv) Library catalogues show location of the document in the library

33. "Festschrift" is a document:

(i) Published on any festival

(ii) Published by an International Agency

(iii) Published in machine readable format

(iv) Published in honour of certain person.

34. Directory of Indian Scientific Periodicals is published from :

(i) NISCAIR

(ii) DESIDOC

(iii) National Library

(iv) Central Reference Library

35. FARMDOC is a service associated with :

(i) Farm products (ii) Plastic products

(iii) Pharmaceuticals (iv) Animal products

36. Meta-book is a term related to:

(i) Books of abnormally large size

(ii) Books written in foreign

(iii) Books of colourful binding

(iv) All non-book language

37. Making the contact of right document to right reader is duty of:

(i) Reference Incharge (ii) Head Librarian

(iii) National Librarian (iv) Circulation Incharge

38. Which documents are known as documents of Nascent Miro-thought?
   (i) Rare documents
   (ii) Grey literature
   (iii) Conference proceedings
   (iv) Periodicals

39. "Cumulative Books Index" is published from:
   (i) UK (ii) USA
   (iii) India (iv) UNESCO

40. Encyclopedia Britannica is published from :
   (i) Chicago (ii) New York
   (iii) Paris (iv) New Jersey

41. Newspaper clippings are used to provide:
   (i) Indexing service (ii) SDI
   (iii) CAS (iv) Abstracting Service

42. Sear's list of subject headings was first published in:
   (i) 1901 (ii) 1920
   (iii) 1923 (iv) 1876

43. "User' Studies" can be any of these types:
   (i) Use Studies
   (ii) Information flow studies
   (iii) Behaviour studies
   (iv) All of the above

44. Lexicography is an art of
   (i) Writing and editing research papers
   (ii) Writing and editing Encyclopedias
   (iii) Writing and editing dictionaries
   (iv) Writing and editing International journals.

45. NUCSSI is a kind of source:
    (i) Informal Source (ii) Primary Source
    (iii) Secondary Source (iv) Tertiary Source

46. "Tertiary documents" is a kind of division of documents, given by:
    (i) S.R. Ranganathan (ii) Denis Grogan
    (iii) C.W. Hanson (iv) Calvin Mooers

47. Who is regarded as 'Father of Bibliography':
    (i) Dr J S Shera (ii) Paul Otlet
    (iii) Konard Gesner (iv) Ranganathan

48. Who is the publisher of "Library Literature"?
    (i) UNECO (ii) R.R. Bowker
    (iii) H.W. Wilson (iv) DRTC

49. What is the frequency of BNB?
    (i) Monthly (ii) Fortnightly
    (iii) Weekly (iv) Bimonthly

50. Which one of the following book will be read from first page to last page?
    (i) Ranganthan's "Five Laws of Library Science".
    (ii) Europa World Yearbook
    (iii) Oxford English Dictionary
    (iv) Encyclopedia of Religion and Ethics

51. Which one of the following is publication of "National Library of Medicine"?
    (i) Index Medicus
    (ii) AGRICOLA
    (iii) Science Citation Index
    (iv) BLAISE

52. Cumulative book index is a publication of :
    (i) America (ii) Paris
    (iii) London (iv) New Delhi

53. Dissertation Abstracts International is published from:
    (i) Paris (ii) Russia
    (iii) U.K. (iv) U.S.A.

54. Information in square brackets in a catalogue card denotes that :
    (i) It is highly authentic
    (ii) It is taken from outside sources
    (iii) It is obsolete
    (iv) None of the above

55. The term Bibliography is derived from:
    (i) Roman word (ii) Latin word
    (iii) Greek word (iv) French word

56. Indian reference manual is a kind of_______ source.
    (i) Primary Source (ii) Secondary Source
    (iii) Tertiary Source (iv) None of the above

57. "Journal of Documentation" is published from:
    (i) Canada (ii) United Kingdom (UK)
    (iii) India (iv) USA

58. Union catalogue, provides information about
    (i) Trade catalogues of different trade unions.
    (ii) Bibliographies of documents published on a country
    (iii) Catalogue of two or more libraries
    (iv) List of books weeded out from a library.

59. Which one of the following is not a micro-film?
    (i) Microfilm (ii) Micro-document
    (iii) Microfiche (iv) Microcard

60. "Documentation and its facets" is written by:
    (i) S.R.Ranganathan (ii) Neelaneghan
    (iii) Henri La Fontaine (iv) S.C. Bradford

61. MAPA is a
    (i) Abstracting Service
    (ii) Monograph Bibliographies
    (iii) Photocopying Services
    (iv) None of the above

62. Which one of the following Indexing System uses 'title' as a single source of information?
    (i) POPSI
    (ii) PRECIS
    (iii) Keyword Indexing System
    (iv) Chain Indexing

63. Which one of the following is an Abstracting Service of Russia?
    (i) DEVSIS
    (ii) Bibliotheque Natonale
    (iii) Referativyni Zhurnal
    (iv) INSPEC

64. "VINIT" is associated with:
    (i) Information Storage
    (ii) Information Retrieval
    (iii) Machine Translation
    (iv) Library Software

65. National Index of Translations (NIT) is published by :
    (i) DESIDOC (ii) NISCAIR
    (iii) BLLD (iv) ASLIB

66. "World Transindex" is published from:
    (i) Chicago (ii) Paris
    (iii) Boston (iv) Netherlands

67. "CAPS" is a service provided by:
    (i) NISCAIR (ii) NISTADS
    (iii) DESIDOC (iv) IFLA

68. Medicinal and Aromatic Plants Abstracts (MAPA) is published by:
    (i) CSIR (ii) UGC
    (iii) ICSSR (iv) NML

69. "Food Technology Abstract" is published by
    (i) Food & Agriculture Organisation (Rome)
    (ii) NISCAIR (new Delhi)
    (iii) NICFOS (Mysore)
    (iv) Library of Congress

70. Bibliotheques et Archive is a division of :
    (i) Library of Congress
    (ii) UNESCO
    (iii) British Museum Library
    (iv) IFLA

71. International Institute of Bibliography is located at:
    (i) Paris (ii) London
    (iii) Chicago (iv) Brussels

72. Documentation Activities can be divided into:
    (i) Advanced documentation activities
    (ii) Active documentation activities
    (iii) Anticipated documentation activities
    (iv) None of these

73. "Literature Search" is a documentation activity under:
    (i) Active documentation activity
    (ii) Advanced documentation activity
    (iii) Passive documentation activity
    (iv) Pre-defined documentation activity

74. BIOSIS is a service in the discipline of :
    (i) Mathematical sciences
    (ii) Physical Sciences
    (iii) Chemical Sciences
    (iv) Biological Sciences

75. Indexing service is provided under:
    (i) Catching-up approach
    (ii) Current approach
    (iii) Everyday approach
    (iv) Exhaustive approach

76. Contents-by-Journal is a kind of :
    (i) CAS
    (ii) SDI
    (iii) Everyday approach
    (iv) None of these

77. COMPENDEX is a indexing service in :
    (i) Chemical services

(ii) Mathematical services
(iii) Engineering & Technology
(iv) Computer Sciences

78. National Technical Information Service (NTIS) is a service of:
(i) U.S.A. (ii) U.K.
(iii) Russia (iv) India

79. The indexes issued with chemical abstract are:
(i) Patent Concordance
(ii) Numerical Patent Index
(iii) Author Index
(iv) All of the above

80. Biological Abstract is issued since:
(i) 1913 (ii) 1927
(iii) 1976 (iv) 1900

81. Excerpta Media (EM) is a kind of :
(i) Indexing Service
(ii) Information Retrieval Services
(iii) Vocabulary Control Device
(iv) Abstracting Services

82. Head Office of BIOSIS service provider is at:
(i) Chicago (ii) Philadelphia
(iii) Kanpur (iv) Hague

83. The new name of UN's "International Referral System" is
(i) UNIRS (ii) INFOTECH
(iii) INFOTERA (iv) INFONET

84. INB divides the documents into following section:
   (i) Government Publications
   (ii) All other publications in all 14 languages
   (iii) Both of the above
   (iv) None of the above

85. Xeroxing of Micro-documents is done by :
   (i) Electrostat method
   (ii) Diazo process
   (iii) Lamination method
   (iv) All of he above

86. PRECIS was developed by
   (i) D.J. Foskett (ii) Derek Austin
   (iii) Pauline Atherton (iv) Neelamegham

87. Science Citation Index (SCI) is published by :
   (i) National Science Library, New Delhi
   (ii) Library of Congress, Washington
   (iii) Institute for Scientific Information, Philadelphia
   (iv) UNESCO

88. Which of the following is not part of computerized SDI?
   (i) Creating a "User Profile"
   (ii) Matching of "User Profile" to "Document Profile"
   (iii) Creating a "Document Profile"
   (iv) Circulating journal articles to research scholars

89. "LISA" falls under the category of

(i) Abstracting Journal
(ii) Indexing Journal
(iii) Subject Heading List
(iv) National bibliography of France

90. BLAISE Stands for
(i) British Library Abstracting Information Service
(ii) British Library Automated Information Service
(iii) British Library Automated Indexing Service
(iv) None of the above

91. Abstract of a document denotes:
(i) Its location
(ii) Concise representation of it
(iii) Bibliographic details
(iv) Details of Publisher

92. Computerized SDI is introduced by
(i) H.P. Luhn (ii) Calvin Mooers
(iii) Mourtiner Taube (iv) Derik Austin

93. Eugene Garfield is pioneer in
(i) Dickman Charging System
(ii) Computerized SDI
(iii) Annotated bibliography
(iv) Citation Indexing

94. Indian National Bibliography (INB) is published from:
(i) National Library, Calcutta
(ii) Central Reference Library, Calcutta
(iii) National Science Library, New Delhi
(iv) Central Secretariat Library, New Delhi

95. Which one of the following is an example of a pre-coordinate indexing?
(i) POPSI (ii) PRECIS
(iii) Chain Indexing (iv) All of the above

96. SCI contains three main indexes, which one of the following is not related to it ?
(i) Citation Index
(ii) Permuterm Subject Index
(iii) Source Index
(iv) Author Index

97. Eugene Garfield, develops his SCI, with the help of ideas from:
(i) Shepard's Citation Index
(ii) Social Science Citation Index
(iii) Price's Citation Index
(iv) None of the above

98. Passive documentation activity is equivalent to:
(i) Documentation work
(ii) Active documentation
(iii) Work carried out in anticipation of demand
(iv) Work carried out in response to user's request.

99. Which classification scheme is used in INB?
(i) UDC (ii) LC
(iii) CC (iv) DDC

100. INB is divided into :
(i) Two parts (ii) Four parts
(iii) Three parts (iv) Six parts

Answer Sheet

1. (iv)	2. (i)	3. (ii)	4. (iii)
5. (i)	6. (iii)	7. (iii)	8. (iii)
9. (i)	10. (iv)	11. (iii)	12. (i)
13. (iv)	14. (ii)	15. (ii)	16. (iii)
17. (iv)	18. (iv)	19. (ii)	20. (iii)
21. (i)	22. (i)	23. (i)	24. (ii)
25. (iv)	26. (i)	27. (iv)	28. (i)
29. (iii)	30. (iii)	31. (iv)	32. (iv)
33. (iv)	34. (i)	35. (iii)	36. (iv)
37. (i)	38. (iv)	39. (ii)	40. (i)
41. (iii)	42. (iii)	43. (iv)	44. (iii)
45. (iv)	46. (ii)	47. (iii)	48. (iii)
49. (iii)	50. (i)	51. (i)	52. (i)
53. (ii)	54. (ii)	55. (iii)	56. (ii)
57. (ii)	58. (iii)	59. (ii)	60. (i)
61. (i)	62. (iii)	63. (iii)	64. (iii)
65. (ii)	66. (iv)	67. (i)	68. (i)
69. (iii)	70. (ii)	71. (iv)	72. (ii)
73. (iii)	74. (iv)	75. (iv)	76. (i)
77. (iii)	78. (i)	79. (iv)	80. (ii)
81. (iv)	82. (ii)	83. (iii)	84. (iii)
85. (ii)	86. (ii)	87. (iii)	88. (iv)
89. (i)	90. (ii)	91. (ii)	92. (i)
93. (iv)	94. (ii)	95. (iv)	96. (iv)
97. (i)	98. (iv)	99. (iv)	100. (i)

Unit-IV

Library Classification & Cataloguing

1. In 1961, "International Conference on cataloguing practices was held at:
   (i) Bangalore (ii) London
   (iii) Chicago (iv) Paris

2. Who is associated with "Rules for a dictionary catalog"
   (i) Panizzi
   (ii) Prof. Charles C.Jewelt
   (iii) C.A. Cutter
   (iv) Andrea Crestadoro

3. Second edition of AACR 2 was first published in:
   (i) 1967 (ii) 1961
   (iii) 1974 (iv) 1978

4. The terms NT, BT and RT are used in
   (i) Vocabulary Control Devices
   (ii) Classified Catalogue Code
   (iii) Classification Schedules
   (iv) Library Statistics Maintenance

5. Library of Congress started MARC project in:
   (i) 1867 (ii) 1978
   (iii) 1966 (iv) 1903

6. "Record Label" of UKMARC is equivalent to ____ USMARC?
   (i) Record Leader
   (ii) Record Label
   (iii) It uses both (i) & (ii)
   (iv) None of these

7. The UNIMARC came into existence in :
   (i) 1967 (ii) 1977
   (iii) 1978 (iv) 1968

8. CCF stands for:
   (i) Common Communication format
   (ii) Committee for communication format
   (iii) Centre for communication format
   (iv) None of these

9. UNIBID is related to :
   (i) Biographical description
   (ii) Biological description
   (iii) Bibliographic description
   (iv) Bibliographic data system

10. Common isolates in UDC are:
    (i) Special & Common auxiliaries
    (ii) ACI & PCI
    (iii) Form divisions & view points
    (iv) Space CI & Time CI

11. Which one of the followings says "Notation is merely a set of symbols sanding in the place of terms".
    (i) Ranganathan (ii) Lancaster
    (iii) Richardson (iv) Sayers

12. CC 6th d. uses phase relation indicator:
    (i) Anpersand (ii) Color
    (iii) Zero (iv) Dot

13. Broad System of Ordering is:
    (i) A catalogue code
    (ii) An indexing technique
    (iii) A classification system
    (iv) None of the above

14. The "Biophysics"' subject has evolved due to:
    (i) Fusion (ii) Fission
    (iii) Cluster (iv) Denundation

15. What does Dichotomy means:
    (i) Division into eight (ii) Division into ten
    (iii) Division into two (iv) Division into four

16. How many levels of phase relations are in colon classification?
    (i) Six (ii) Four
    (iii) One (iv) Three

17. The word catalogue is derived from the word kat lagos of:
    (i) French (ii) Latin
    (iii) Greek (iv) Chinese

18. British Museum code is related to :
    (i) Ranganathan (ii) Richardson
    (iii) Sayers (iv) Panizzi

19. A list which shows the arrangement of documents in the library?
    (i) Accession List (ii) Shelf list

(iii) Call Number (iv) Class Number

20. Thesaurus is a kind of indexing languages:
(i) Natural (ii) Controlled
(iii) Free (iv) All the above

21. "Nothing before something" filing method is also known as:
(i) Letter by letter (ii) Word by word
(iii) Both of the above (iv) None of the above

22. How many categories of Indexing languages are common:
(i) Two (ii) Five
(iii) Six (iv) One

23. Prenatal cataloguing is given by:
(i) Sayers (ii) Lancester
(iii) Ranganathan (iv) Richardson

24. Which one indicate inner form of the catalogue:
(i) Classified catalogue
(ii) Book Catalogue
(iii) Card catalogue
(iv) Shelf list

25. "Library of Congress filing rules" was published in:
(i) 1956 (ii) 1967
(iii) 1978 (iv) 1901

26. Which one of the following revised and edited 7th Ed. Of Colon classification?
(i) S.R. Ranganathan (ii) M.A. Gopinath
(iii) G. Bhattacharya (iv) Neelaneghan

27. "Whole-organ" principle comes under:
    (i) Principle of helpful sequence
    (ii) Caronical sequence
    (iii) Principle of facts sequence
    (iv) None of the above

28. The Botany in DDC is arranged according to :
    (i) Principle of Later in Evolution
    (ii) Principle of Earlier in Evaluation
    (iii) Principle of Later in Time
    (iv) Principle of Earlier in Time

29. The "Medicine" in CC 6th Ed. Follows:
    (i) Principle of Bottom Upwards
    (ii) Principle of Top down words
    (iii) Principle of Later-in-time
    (iv) Principle of later in evolution

30. When a number is written in square brackets in DDC it indicates?
    (i) Number is vacant (ii) For special use
    (iii) No more in use (iv) None of the above

31. A MARC record consist of _____ main sections:
    (i) Eight (ii) Six
    (iii) Four (iv) Three

32. Relative Index is related to :
    (i) DDC (ii) EC
    (iii) CC (iv) BSO

33. In AACR-2, the rendering of the Gregg R. Notes as author will be:
    (i) Notess, Gregg R (ii) Notess, Gregg R

(iii) Notess (Gregg R) (iv) Notess, (Gregg R)

34. MARC stands for :
(i) Machine Readable Catalogue,
(ii) Machine Readable Cataloging
(iii) Machine reading Catalogue
(iv) None of these

35. Chain Indexing was developed by:
(i) S.R. Ranganathan
(ii) Lancaster
(iii) Neelameghan & Bhattacharya
(iv) Derek Austin

36. Chain Indexing was initially used:
(i) INB (ii) SCI
(iii) POPSI (iv) BNB

37. MeSH is an example of :
(i) Subject Headings List
(ii) Classification Schedule
(iii) Abstracting Journal
(iv) None of the above

38. First edition of DDC consisted of:
(i) 2 volumes (ii) 44 pages
(iii) 144 pages (iv) 4 volumes

39. J. Coramani was editor of :
(i) 21st edition of DDC
(ii) 7th edition of CC
(iii) 18th edition of Sear's list
(iv) 21st edition of LCSH

40. UDC was designed in
    (i) 1876 (ii) 1978
    (iii) 1903 (iv) 1905

41. UNIBID is an agency associated with:
    (i) Biographic Description
    (ii) Bibliographic Description
    (iii) Classification Schemes
    (iv) Subject headings list

42. Which one of the following is not a plane defined by Dr.S.R. Ranganathan?
    (i) Verbal Plane (ii) Idea Plane
    (iii) Notational Plane (iv) Vertical Plane

43. 6th edition of colon classification was published in:
    (i) 1972 (ii) 1976
    (iii) 1967 (iv) 1960

44. Expansive classification was devised by :
    (i) Antono Panizzi (ii) C.A.Cutter
    (iii) Melvil Dewey (iv) Neelameghan

45. The sequence of steps taken in Analytico-synthetic classification schemes are:
    (i) Facet Synthesize – Facet Sequence – Facet Analyses
    (ii) Facet Analysis – Facet Numbering –Facet Sequence
    (iii) Facet Analysis – Facet Sequence
    (iv) None of the above

46. Out of five fundamental categories, which one is highly concrete?

(i) Energy (ii) Personality
(iii) Space (iv) Time

47. "Principle of Inversion" is followed in
(i) Subject Headings derivation
(ii) Indexing of scientific periodicals
(iii) Abstracting of Social Science periodicals
(iv) Classifying and arranging of documents.

48. Postulational approach to classification gives principles for:
(i) Facet Analysis and Synthesis
(ii) Selecting terminology of index terms
(iii) Rendering subject headings in a catalogue
(iv) Arranging documents on shelves.

49. 7th Edition of colon classification contains _____ number of Basic Subjects:
(i) 669 (ii) 679
(iii) 769 (iv) 779

50. "Biotechnology" is formed as a result of :
(i) Fusion (ii) Fission
(iii) Agglomeration (iv) Lamination

51. "Clustering" is a term associated with:
(i) Modes of Subject formation
(ii) Modes of Information Storage
(iii) Modes of communication
(iv) Modes of knowledge dissemination

52. Who was first Education Minister of Independent India.
(i) Dr. S. Radhakrishnan

(ii) Dr.C.D. Deshmukh

(iii) Dr.Zakir Husain

(iv) Maulana Abul Kalam Azad

53. The standard size of card catalogue is:

(i) 7.5 x 5.3 cm (ii) 7.3 x 5.3 inch

(iii) 5.3 x 7.3 cm (iv) 5.3 x 7.3 mm

54. "CRIE" and "BIE" terms are related to :

(i) Colon classification

(ii) AACR-2 (Rev.) edition

(iii) Panizi's Catalogue code

(iv) Classified catalogue code

55. Recall and Relevance are related to :

(i) Cataloguing

(ii) Classficiation

(iii) Natural Language Indexing

(iv) Information Retrieval

56. Which one of the following is now publisher of DDC?

(i) Melvil Dewey Endowment of Library Science

(ii) S.Ranganathan Endowment of Library Science

(iii) Forest Press Inc.

(iv) OCLC Inc.

57. "Library Journal" was published for the first time in :

(i) 1876 (ii) 1800

(iii) 1976 (iv) 1899

58. Dynamic Theory of Library classification is associated with?
    (i) Dr.S.R. Ranganathan
    (ii) Lancaster
    (iii) W.B. Sayers
    (iv) Melvil Dewey

59. Dr. S.R. Ranganathan is associated with publication of :
    (i) Colon classification – 7th Edition
    (ii) Journal of Library & Information Science
    (iii) General Theory of Library Classification
    (iv) Prolegomena to library classification.

60. How many modes of subject formation were initially given by Ranganathan?
    (i) Four (ii) Fourteen
    (iii) Five (iv) Three

61. "Homeopathy" is taken as____ in colon classification:
    (i) Systems (ii) Subject Bundles
    (iii) Specials (iv) Aqatomerates

62. 7th Edition of colon classification arranges Main subjects by following principle of :
    (i) Decreasing predictability and Increasing contents richness.
    (ii) Less known subjects to well-known subjects
    (iii) First come & First serve
    (iv) None of the above.

63. Out of "Systems" and "Specials" in a classification scheme which one is given preference?

(i) Systems
(ii) Specials
(iii) Both Simultaneously
(iv) None of these

64. Homonym is defined as :
(i) Two words having same spelling.
(ii) Two words giving two different meanings
(iii) Two words giving same meanings
(iv) Same word giving different meanings.

65. Canon of context is related to:
(i) Idea plane (ii) Verbal plane
(iii) Notational plane (iv) None of these

66. "Minor Authors" initially used in DDC was removed due to the effect of:
(i) Canon of Reference
(ii) Canon of Permanence
(iii) Canon of context
(iv) Canon of currency

67. What is "Base" in a Notational System?
(i) A paper which have digits written on it.
(ii) Total digits available in a notational system.
(iii) A set of digits used by a notational system.
(iv) None of these.

68. Library of Congress uses:
(i) Non-faceted notation
(ii) Pure notation
(iii) Roman Smalls
(iv) Indo-Arabic notation

69. Place value of 6 in 0.635 is:
    (i) 6000 (ii) 600
    (iii) 7/1000 (iv) 6/10

70. The residual class in DDC is denoted by digit:
    (i) 9 (ii) 8
    (iii) 0 (iv) None of these

71. ISBD divides elements in a bibliographic description into:
    (i) 7-areas (ii) 8-areas
    (iii) 17-areas (iv) 71-areas

72. Which punctuation sign will be used before subtitle AACR-2?
    (i) Colon (ii) Semi-colon
    (iii) Dash (iv) Dot

73. In AACR-2, which level of description provides maximum information:
    (i) First (ii) Third
    (iii) Second (iv) None of these

74. Which link in chain indexing is used as a subject heading?
    (i) Sought link (ii) Missing link
    (iii) False link (iv) Unsought link

75. The "Cycle Indexing" is developed by
    (i) S.R. Ranganathan (ii) Lancaster
    (iii) D.J. Foskett (iv) M.E. Sears

76. H.P. Luhn is related to :
    (i) POPSI (ii) PRECIS
    (iii) KWOC (iv) KWIC

77. Designer of Classification Scheme is:
(i) Classifier (ii) Classificationist
(iii) Classes (iv) Class

78. Chain procedure divides links into:
(i) Significant links (ii) Insignificant links
(iii) Both of the above (iv) None of the above

79. AACR-1 defines series as:
(i) A list of documents published by a publisher in a year
(ii) A number of separate books published in succession and related to one another by a collective title.
(iii) Proceedings of government legislatures
(iv) None of the above

80. ISBD (M) is associated with bibliographic description of:
(i) Motion pictures (ii) Maps
(iii) Monographs (iv) Monograms

81. Which one of the following punctuation sign is not used in AACR-2?
(i) Plus sign (ii) Colon
(iii) Semi-colon (iv) Asterik

82. Which classification scheme is used in classifying ISA?
(i) LC (ii) CC
(iii) UDC (iv) DDC

83. In AACR-2, a _____ is used before the first statement of responsibility that comes after the title?

(i) Comma (ii) Semi-colon
(iii) Diagonal Slash (iv) Two dots

84. "Three dots" are used in AACR-2
(i) After Indian Authors name in main entry.
(ii) Indicates Omissions
(iii) Inserted after parallel titles.
(iv) Inserted after each element in the tracing.

85. AACR-2 provides, how many types of levels of description?
(i) Four (ii) Two
(iii) Three (iv) One

86. Which one of the following catalogue is used in stock verification?
(i) Inventory catalogue
(ii) Union catalogue
(iii) Card catalogue
(iv) MARC form catalogue

87. Which one of the following is associated with British Museum Library?
(i) C.A. Culter (ii) Lancaster
(iii) Antony Panizzi (iv) None

88. Which one of the following author's name is not inverted?
(i) English names
(ii) Name of female authors
(iii) Ethiopian names
(iv) Indic names

89. Entry element is defined as:
    (i) Word or groups of words occurring first in the heading
    (ii) Name/Title under which main entry is made
    (iii) Name of the catalogue, who has made its entry.
    (iv) It is a concept in documents which have fancy titles.

90. Transliteration of any author name helps in:
    (i) It's cataloging by the non-English knowing catalogues.
    (ii) It's understanding by a common library user
    (iii) It's alphabetical arrangement
    (iv) None of the above

91. Which punctuation sign is used when author's name is inverted?
    (i) Comma (ii) Semi-colon
    (iii) Colon (iv) Dot

92. In ISBD (G) the alphabet (G) stands for:
    (i) Graphs (ii) Geometrical
    (iii) Geographical (iv) General

93. "Coordinate Indexing" is also known as:
    (i) Pre-coordinate Indexing
    (ii) Post-coordinate Indexing
    (iii) PRECIS
    (iv) UNITERM Indexing technique

94. 5th edition, of CCC by Ranganathan was published in:
    (i) 1964 (ii) 1972

(iii) 1938 (iv) 1998

95. When coordination of index terms is done at selection of document, then it is:
    (i) Keyword-out-of-context (KWOC)
    (ii) Pre-coordinate indexing
    (iii) It is not a indexing technique
    (iv) Post coordinate indexing

96. Which edition of colon classification is freely faceted classification.
    (i) Edition -1 (ii) Edition -2
    (iii) Edition-6 (iv) Edition-7

97. The "Library Journal" publishes its first issue in:
    (i) 1976 (ii) 1876
    (iii) 1901 (iv) 1900

98. Who was the first editor of "Library Journal" ?
    (i) Melvil Dewey (ii) S.R.Ranganathan
    (iii) Berwick Sayers (iv) C.A.Cutter

99. The 20th edition of DDC came in:
    (i) 1978 (ii) 1979
    (iii) 1981 (iv) 1989

100. Double colon in UDC is used to show:
    (i) Simple relation
    (ii) Subgrouping
    (iii) Order fixing
    (iv) coordination

101. In a classification system we are not bothered about:

(i) Place value of digit
(ii) Ordinal value of digit
(iii) Coordinal value of digit
(iv) Semantic value of digit

102. Which of the following deices are used to increase the capacity of a notational system?
(i) Octave device (ii) sector device
(iii) Packeted notation (iv) All of the above

103. C.C.C. is divided into:
(i) 26 parts (ii) 2 parts
(iii) 21 parts (iv) 20 parts

104. C.C.C. (5th ed) is divided on the basis of :
(i) Five Criteria (ii) Three Criteria
(iii) Six Criteria (iv) Two Criteria

105. In CCC, CIE and CRIE are described in:
(i) Part A to D (ii) Part G
(iii) Part K & L (iv) Part S-W

106. Which one of the following is not a criteria in division of CCC (5th Ed)?
(i) Normative principles and theory
(ii) Cataloging operations
(iii) Types of entries
(iv) Rules of choice of access points

107. In CCC, entry can be made in title only when:
(i) It is a government publication
(ii) When there are more than three author?
(iii) When there is no author or collaborator
(iv) Entry can never be in title of document

108. In AACR-2, entry can be in the name of collaborator, if :
   (i) here are more collaborators than its authors
   (ii) The collaborators are of high repute
   (iii) If the document is government publication
   (iv) It can never be in the name of collaborator

109. Which cataloguing code, denies to take information about entry element from outside source?
   (i) AACRI (ii) AACR-II
   (iii) CCC (iv) AA

110. In AACR-2, entry is made under title when:
   (i) Document is produced by three authors.
   (ii) Document is a Non-book material
   (iii) Document is having fancy title
   (iv) Document is a sacred scripture

111. In CCC, anonymous work is entered under:
   (i) Title of the document
   (ii) Name of the publisher
   (iii) Name of the collaborator
   (iv) No clear roles are there

112. "A tale of tub (published anonymously, by J.Swift" will be entered under ____ in CCC.
   (i) Title
   (ii) Swift, J
   (iii) Swift, J, with Reference entry under title
   (iv) None of the above

113. If the title page of the document does not gives the name of personal author, which one of the

following will be used first in main entry heading?
(i) Title of the document
(ii) Name of the joint collaborators
(iii) Name of the collaborator
(iv) Name of the publisher

114. Standard size of Sheaf Catalogue is:
(i) 18.5 x 7.5 cm (ii) 10 x 12.5 cm
(iii) 18.5 x 10 cm (iv) 12.5 x 7.5 cm

115. "See" reference entry is related to :
(i) CCC (ii) AACR-2
(iii) Both of the above (iv) None of the above

116. First edition of "Sears list of subject heading was published in :
(i) 1923 (ii) 1933
(iii) 1986 (iv) 1876

117. "Theory of Library Catalogue" was written by :
(i) C.A. Cutter (ii) Marget Mann
(iii) S.R. Ranganathan (iv) Lancaster

118. Which one of the following is most accepted physical form of catalogue?
(i) Card form (ii) Book Form
(iii) Sheaf Form (iv) MARC form

119. In AACR-2, a reference entry is to be made when:
(i) Author of a document is not ascertained.
(ii) There are anonymous editions of works whose authors have been ascertained.
(iii) When there is a government publication.
(iv) When document is in machine readable form.

120. "Portability" is a characteristic while studying:
 (i) During choice of subject headings.
 (ii) Comparison of AACR-2 and CCC
 (iii) Inner form of Catalogue
 (iv) Physical form of catalogue

121. How many zones have been identified by Dr Ranganathan in an array:
 (i) 3 (ii) 5
 (iii) 4 (iv) 6

122. Which National Library is associated with AACR-I :
 (i) National Library of India
 (ii) British Museum
 (iii) Library of Congress
 (iv) State Lenin Library

123. All through alphabetization is also known as :
 (i) Letter by letter (ii) Word by word
 (iii) Both of these (iv) None of these

124. Classified cataloguing code was developed by:
 (i) Dr.S.R. Ranganathan
 (ii) Melvil Dewey
 (iii) C.A. Cutter
 (iv) Wilson & Taube

125. ISBDs are brought out by:
 (i) ALA (ii) LA
 (iii) IFLA (iv) UNESCO

126. AACR-2, main entry is in title when:

(i) Tile of document is beautifully written
(ii) Document is a government document
(iii) When there are more than three authors and nine of them is principal
(iv) None of these

127. Which of the following international document initially uses chain procedure?
(i) INB
(ii) Sear's list of subject heading
(iii) INSPEC
(iv) BNB

128. Which one of the following visible indexes uses cards in it?
(i) Lindex (ii) Chaindex
(iii) Stripdex (iv) Kardex

129. Which one of the following uses words of tiles in deriving subject headings?
(i) KWIC (ii) KWAC
(iii) KWOC (iv) All of the above

130. Subject analytical entry is known in CCC as:
(i) CIE (ii) BIE
(iii) CRIE (iv) CRE

131. If the main entry in AACR-2 is under title, then added entry will be under:
(i) Any collaborator (ii) Publisher
(iii) Both of these (iv) None of these

132. Ranganathan does not give emphasis on Imprint & Collation because :

(i) Ranganathan was not aware of these terms.

(ii) Ranganathan cannot give attention to terms

(iii) Ranganathan gives emphasis on closed access.

(iv) Ranganathan considered that catalogue of open access does not need such sections.

133. In CCC, short form for 'Editor' is

(i) Ed. (ii) Edit.

(iii) ed. (iv) None of the above

134. Which one of the following journal was published by Ranganathan?

(i) Annals of Library Science

(ii) Library science with a slant to documentation

(iii) Journal of Lib. & Inf. Science

(iv) None of the above

135. According to AACR-2, if a person is known by different names, then main entry will be in :

(i) Latest name

(ii) Name that appears most frequently in his/her works

(iii) Both of these will be considered

(iv) None of these

136. Which one of the following term is given by Ranganathan?

(i) Cooperative cataloguing

(ii) Centralised cataloguing

(iii) Literary warrant

(iv) Pre-natal cataloguing

137. Links representing connecting symbols is known as:

(i) False links (ii) Missing links
(iii) Sought links (iv) Unsought links

138. Unsought links are those links:

(i) Which represents relationship isolates
(ii) Which are used by readers in searching documents
(iii) Which represents subjects but not sought by readers
(iv) None of the above

139. In using chain procedure, the classification scheme should have:

(i) Indo-Arabic Notation
(ii) The lower link in it must be a sub-division of its above link
(iii) It should have any type fo facet sequence.
(iv) It should be purely enumerative scheme.

140. Library of Congress initiated the following programme:

(i) Pre-natal cataloguing
(ii) Cataloguing-in-publication
(iii) Both of the above
(iv) None of the above

141. Canon of Ascertainability is proposed by:

(i) Antony Panizzi (ii) S.R. Ranganathan
(iii) C.A. Cutter (iv) H.P. Luhn

142. S.R. Ranganathan gives _______ canons of cataloguing:

(i) Six (ii) Three
(iii) Five (iv) Nine

143. Which on of the following canons is most important in choice of headings?
(i) Cannon of Sought Headings
(ii) Canon of Ascertainability
(iii) Cannon of context
(iv) Canon of currency

144. In AACR-2, first part deals with :
(i) History of AACR-2
(ii) Description of Non-book materials
(iii) Choice and rendering of headings
(iv) Descriptive cataloguing

145. Non-book materials is dealt in AACR-I at:
(i) Part-I (ii) Part-III
(iii) Part-IV (iv) Part-II

146. AACR-2 is divided into :
(i) Is a single document
(ii) Three parts
(iii) Two parts
(iv) Six parts

147. AACR-1 was divided into :
(i) One part (ii) Three parts
(iii) Two parts (iv) Four parts

148. Chapter-I (Part-I) in AACR-2 is related to :
(i) Descriptive cataloguing applicable to non-book materials.
(ii) Descriptive cataloguing applicable to any

kind of lib. material

(iii) Both of the above

(iv) None of the above

149. Chapter 2-13 (Part-I) in AACR-2 are related to :

(i) Descriptive cataloguing of Government publications.

(ii) Descriptive cataloguing of conference proceedings.

(iii) Descriptive cataloguing of specific types of lib. materials

(iv) None of the above

150. Which edition of AACR gives more illustration examples?

(i) AACR-I

(ii) AACR-II

(iii) Both gives similar emphasis

(iv) None gives any examples.

151. "Choice of Access points" is dealt at ___ in AACR-2 :

(i) Part-I (ii) Part-II

(iii) Both have its rules (iv) None of these

152. 'Part M' in CCC is most important because of :

(i) It gives theoretical aspects of cataloguing.

(ii) It is related to non-book materials.

(iii) It gives Ranganathan's biography

(iv) Rules for choice & rendering of main entries.

153. "Geographic Names" in AACR-2 is dealt at :

(i) Chapter-12 (ii) Chapter-13

(iii) Chapter-21 (iv) Chapter-23

154. In AACR-2, Part-I is further sub-divided into:

(i) 3-chapters (ii) 6-chapters

(iii) 13 – chapters (iv) 20-chapters

155. While choosing main entry heading, what is main difference in AACR-2 and CCC.

(i) In AACR-2 information can be taken from outside source

(ii) In CCC, information can be sought from other sources

(iii) Both of the above

(iv) No difference in AACR-2 and CCC.

156. In Canon of Recall value, Recall value means.

(i) Word which a documents repeats in its title.

(ii) Word which a user uses in its day-to-day life.

(iii) Word that is most likely to be back to the memory by a user.

(iv) None of the above.

157. Which cannon prescribes that the current usage term should be used in describing subject in subject entries?

(i) Canon of sought headings.

(ii) Canon of permanence

(iii) Canon of context

(iv) Canon of currency

158. Which canon says that heading in a catalogue entry should not be subjected to change?

(i) Canon of Individualization

(ii) Canon of context

(iii) Canon of currency

(iv) Canon of Permanence

159. How many normative principles are related to cataloguing?
   (i) Three (ii) Four
   (iii) Nine (iv) Six

160. AACR-2 is based on the following principles:
   (i) Principle of Authorship
   (ii) Principle of Literary units
   (iii) Both of he above
   (iv) None of the above

161. Which one of the following canon was added in 1968?
   (i) Canon of context
   (ii) Canon of Sought headings
   (iii) Canon of currency
   (iv) Canon of Recall value.

162. Since when BNB has started using PRECIS in its subject heading derivations:
   (i) 1958 (ii) 1967
   (iii) 1971 (iv) 1978

163. Chain procedure was initiated in:
   (i) 1933 (ii) 1930
   (iii) 1938 (iv) 1935

164. Which canon describes that the most important word group should be used as the entry element?
   (i) Canon of Permanence
   (ii) Canon of Sought Headings
   (iii) Canon of Currency
   (iv) Canon of Prepotence

165. In AACR-2, series area begins after:
   (i) Physical description area
   (ii) Tracing Area
   (iii) ISSN Area
   (iv) Year of Publication

166. Out of the four ISBN components which one is not from it?
   (i) Group Identifier (ii) Year Identifier
   (iii) Publisher Identifier (iv) Title Identifier

167. GMD in AACR-2 stands for:
   (i) General Monographic Details
   (ii) Graphs, Maps Description
   (iii) General Material Description
   (iv) None of these

168. The information about GMD is given in :
   (i) Physical description area
   (ii) Title and responsibility area
   (iii) Tracing area
   (iv) Not given in library catalogue

169. ISSN consist of:
   (i) 6-digits (ii) 8-digits
   (iii) 10-digits (iv) 15-digits

170. ISBN consists of :
   (i) 6-digits (ii) 8-digits
   (iii) 10-digits (iv) 15-digits

171. Standard Book Numbers were used in :
   (i) U.K. (ii) U.S.A.
   (iii) China (iv) India

172. CODATA is associated with :
    (i) Information Retrieval
    (ii) Bibliographic description
    (iii) Indexing system
    (iv) Data compilation

173. In PRECIS, Action is defined by role operator:
    (i) 0 (ii) 1
    (iii) 2 (iv) 6

174. ISBN consists of _____ components
    (i) Three (ii) Five
    (iii) One (iv) Four

175. The elementary categories used in POPSI are written as (in sequence)
    (i) D, E, A, P (ii) D, A, E, P
    (iii) P, D, A, E (iv) P, E, D, A

176. Who is the developer of SLIC index?
    (i) E.J. Coates (ii) J. Kaiser
    (iii) A.C. Foskett (iv) J.R. Sharp

177. Which one of the following is Kaiser's dual category in indexing system?
    (i) Action (ii) Property
    (iii) process (iv) Entity

178. Ideas of E.J. Coates can be seen in the following document:
    (i) Atomindex
    (ii) Current Technology Index
    (iii) Index Medicos'
    (iv) POPSI

179. Mortimer Taube is associated with :
(i) PRECIS (ii) SLIC Index
(iii) UNITERM System (iv) Batten System

180. Zator system is developed by:
(i) Calvin Mooers (ii) Cordonnier
(iii) Mortimer Taube (iv) Derek Austin

181. Optical coincidence system is a type of :
(i) Pre-coordinate indexing
(ii) Post-coordinate indexing
(iii) is not related to indexing system
(iv) None of the above

182. (RT) in thesaurus is used for :
(i) Related term (ii) Right term
(iii) Referred term (iv) Received term

183. The full form of TEST is :
(i) The Engineering science thesaurus
(ii) Thesaurus of Engineering and Scientific terms
(iii) Thesaurus of Scientific & Technology information
(iv) The English subject Thesaurus

184. The main parts of thesaurofacet are:
(i) Thesaurus & faceted classification scheme.
(ii) Subject heading list & classification schedule.
(iii) Both of these are used
(iv) None of these

185. The basic difference between thesaurus and list of subject headings is:

(i) List of subject headings provide simple listing.

(ii) List of subject headings is for post coordinate indexing

(iii) Thesaurus list terms in a helpful order.

(iv) Thesaurus is due to pre-coordinate indexing need.

186. "Precision ratio" is a term used in :

(i) Indexing system

(ii) Evaluation of indexing system

(iii) Information storage devices

(iv) None of these

187. Which one of the following is Recall Oriented device.

(i) Coordiantion (ii) Links

(iii) Roles (iv) Synonym Control

188. Which one of the following is Precision Oriented device?

(i) Word form control (ii) Synonym control

(iii) Coordination (iv) Facet Analysis

189. INIS Thesaurus is a product of :

(i) BARC (Thrombay) (ii) UNESCO (Paris)

(iii) IAEA (Vienna) (iv) NMZ (Washington)

190. Problem of Homonyms is related to :

(i) Artificial Language (ii) Natural Language

(iii) Machine Language (iv) Controlled Language

191. Ranganathan uses (-irt) is his indexes for:

(i) Information retrieval techniques

(ii) Information recall technology

(iii) In relation to

(iv) In relation for

192. Which indexing technique uses keywords outside the title of the document?

(i) KWIC (ii) KWOC

(iii) PRECIS (iv) KWAC

193. The name of J. Kaiser is associated to:

(i) Cataloguing code

(ii) Abstracting technique

(iii) Classification scheme

(iv) Indexing technique

194. What is frequency of printed chemical Abstract?

(i) Monthly (ii) Weekly

(iii) Fortnightly (iv) Quarterly

195. Which one of the following is a post-coordinate indexing system?

(i) PRECIS (ii) POPSI

(iii) KWIC (iv) UNITERM system

196. MeSH is a :

(i) Thesaurus

(ii) Subject heading list

(iii) Classification scheme

(iv) None of these

197. Subject headings along with their relationships are defined in :

(i) Subject headings list

(ii) Encyclopedias

(iii) Dictionaries
(iv) Thesaurus

198. How many indentions are there in AACR-2 ?
(i) Thee (ii) Two
(iii) One (iv) Four

199. Tracing of an entry is done in CCC:
(i) in the last lines of the card.
(ii) In the reverse side of the entry
(iii) In both the places
(iv) Not done in CCC.

200. Illustrative material of a document is given in:
(i) Imprint section
(ii) Collation section
(iii) GMD section
(iv) Physical description section

201. Accession Number in AACR-2 is written:
(i) Along with call number
(ii) At fourth horizontal line from above
(iii) At fourth horizontal line from below
(iv) It not written at all.

202. If we say 9-Apples, then the digit 9 has :
(i) Ordinal value (ii) Cardinal value
(iii) Semantic value (iv) Place value

203. Which of the following principles are related to static theory of classification?
(i) Richardson's criteria
(ii) Bliss's principles

(iii) Berwick Sayer's canons
(iv) All of the above

204. Problem of homonym occurs in:
(i) Idea plane (ii) Verbal plane
(iii) Notational plane (iv) Both (ii)& (iii)

205. Which canon of classification says that the characteristic applied for division of a universe should completely divided it?
(i) Canon of consistent succession
(ii) Canon of Exclusiveness
(iii) Canon of Exhaustiveness
(iv) Canon of Consistent sequence

206. Which canon of classification says that the arrangement of classes in an array of classes should be helpful to the uses?
(i) Canon of Relevant succession
(ii) Canon of consistent succession
(iii) Canon of consistent sequence
(iv) Canon of Helpful sequence

207. Principles of Helpful sequence are related to :
(i) Classification
(ii) Indexing
(iii) Cataloguing
(iv) Information Retrieval

208. An "Array" is defined as:
(i) The classes derived from a universe on the basis of single character.
(ii) The classes derived fro two universe on the basis of single character.

(iii) The classes which cannot be divided on the

209. The totality of the ideas conserved by humans is called :

(i) Idea (ii) Array

(iii) Knowledge (iv) Subject

210. Macro-subject can be defined as :

(i) A subject with huge literature on it.

(ii) A subject having very important aspect.

(iii) A subject whose name is very long

(iv) A subject with great extension and small intensions.

211. "Child marriage" is a type of subject:

(i) Basic subject (ii) Compound subject

(iii) Complex subject (iv) All of the above

212. A generic term used to denote any component of a compound subject.

(i) Facet (ii) Idea

(iii) Focus (iv) Chain

213. Which one of the following is not a metal faculty on which Francis Bacon divides his scheme?

(i) Memory (ii) Intuition

(iii) Imagination (iv) Reason

214. Bodlein library initially uses the classification scheme of:

(i) Melvil Dewey (ii) S.R. Ranganathan

(iii) Francis Bacon (iv) K.V. Gesner

215. Dewey Decimal classification was devised in:

(i) 1814 (ii) 1714
(iii) 1800 (iv) 1876

216. Library of Congress classification was devised in:
(i) 1900 (ii) 1901
(iii) 1801 (iv) 1876

217. Relative index to DDC was included in :
(i) First edition
(ii) Second edition
(iii) Third edition
(iv) Is not its part even today

218. Callimachus is associated with :
(i) Information retrieval
(ii) Classification
(iii) Cataloguing
(iv) Library administration

219. J.C. Brunet belongs to :
(i) France (ii) London
(iii) New York (iv) Russia

220. Which of the following classification schemes have no logical basis?
(i) Baconian system
(ii) Konrad Von Gesner Scheme
(iii) Gabriel Naude's bibliographic classification
(iv) Melvil Dewey's DDC.

221. Who is associated with "Biblitheca Universalis"?
(i) J.C. Brunet (ii) Melvil Dewey
(iii) Gabriel naude (iv) K.V. Gesner

222. Who publishes his classification scheme in "Advancement of Human Learning"
    (i) Francis Bacon (ii) Melvil Dewey
    (iii) S.R. Ranganathan (iv) C.A. Cutter

223. The term "classis" from which classification is derived is a :
    (i) Latin word (ii) French word
    (iii) english word (iv) Russian word

224. The term APUPA was used in his work by:
    (i) B.C. "Vickerey
    (ii) J.S. Mill
    (iii) Dr. S.R. Ranganathan
    (iv) W.C. Berwick Sayers

225. "Kama" is the division of knowledge in
    (i) Comte's classification
    (ii) Baconian classification
    (iii) Greek classification
    (iv) Vedic classification

226. Who said that "Knowledge classification" is the basis of "Library classification"?
    (i) W.C. Berwick Sayers
    (ii) S.R. Ranganathan
    (iii) August Comte
    (iv) Herbert Spenser

227. Which classification scheme follows inverted Baconian classification scheme?
    (i) Bliss classification
    (ii) Colon Classification

(iii) Library of Congress

(iv) DDC

228. In AACR-2, if there are two or three joint author the main entry will be under:
(i) Title of the document
(ii) In all the given authors jointly
(iii) In the first author
(iv) Will be in the name of editor

229. When place of publication is not given in AACR-2, then ____ is used?
(i) S.n. (ii) S.l.
(iii) Thee dots (iv) Left blank

230. If more than one place of publication is given for a document, then in entry _____
(i) Place of international repute will be written.
(ii) S.N. will be written
(iii) First place of publication will be written
(iv) None of these will be used.

231. Which one of the following is correct AACR-2 entry:
(i) India, Human Resource Development, Ministry of
(ii) India, Ministry of Human Resource Development
(iii) India, Parliament of, MHRD
(iv) Any, one of these

232. In the glossing of CCC (rirt) stands for:
(i) Right in relation to
(ii) related in right term

(iii) referred in relation to

(iv) None of these

233. North Indian name is to be entered under the family name in:

(i) AACR-2

(ii) CCC

(iii) In both AACR-2 & CCC

(iv) In None of them

234. The entry element is written in CAPITAL letters in:

(i) AACR-1
(ii) AACR-2
(iii) CCC
(iv) None of these

235. Which indic names are to entered in their first part of the name?

(i) Sikhs
(ii) Muslms
(iii) Bengalis
(iv) North Indians

236. Chapter-23 of AACR-2 deals with :

(i) Choice of Access points

(ii) Headings for persons

(iii) Geographic names

(iv) Uniform titles

237. Chapter-23 of AACR-2 is equivalent to ____ of CCC.

(i) Chapter-MA
(ii) Chapter-JA
(iii) Chapter-MK
(iv) Chapter-JB

238. In AACR-2, the Conference proceeding entry will be

(i) Title (No. of Conf. : Year: Place)

(ii) Title (Year: Place: No. of Conf.)

(iii) Title only.

(iv) (Year: Place: No. of Conf.) Title.

239. The last edition of colon classification was published in:

(i) 1976 (ii) 1987

(iii) 1989 (iv) 2004

240. "Agglomeration" is also known as:

(i) Distillation Kind 1

(ii) Distillation Kind 2

(iii) Lamination

(iv) Partial Comprehension

241. Name of 'B.C. Vikery' is associated with:

(i) Vocabulary control

(ii) Library computerization

(iii) Abstracting rules

(iv) Indexing techniques

242. APUPA is an acronym used in:

(i) Cataloguing process

(ii) Vocabulary control

(iii) Classification of documents

(iv) Reference queries

243. Which one of the following is not a kind of subject?

(i) Simple subject

(ii) Complex subject

(iii) Compound subject

(iv) Duplex subject

244. Margaret Mann is associated with
    (i) Classification
    (ii) Cataloguing
    (iii) Information storage & Retrieval
    (iv) Public Library Movement in USA

245. Which of the following is fully enumerative classification scheme?
    (i) Colon classification
    (ii) Universal Decimal Classification
    (iii) Dewey Decimal Classification
    (iv) Library of Congress Classification

246. From which edition DDC is available online
    (i) 19th Ed. (ii) 20th Ed.
    (iii) 22nd Ed. (iv) 24th Ed.

247. Call Number of a book consist of :
    (i) Class Number (ii) Book Number
    (iii) Collection Number (iv) All of the above

248. Dewey Decimal Classification (DD) is an example of :
    (i) Fully – enumerative classification scheme
    (ii) Rigidly – faceted classification scheme.
    (iii) Almost enumerative classification scheme.
    (iv) Open ended classification scheme.

249. Which one of the following editors is related to both AACR-1 and AACR-2 editing?
    (i) Paul Winkler (ii) Michael Gorman
    (iii) Peter R. Lewis (iv) None of these

250. Which is the latest DDC edition?

(i) 23rd (ii) 21st

(iii) 22nd (iv) 25th

251. The term "Literally warrant" was coined by -

(i) Allan Borden (ii) W.C.B. Sayers

(iii) H.P. Luhn (iv) W. Hulme

252. The 19th edition of DDC consist of :

(i) 3 Auxillary tables (ii) 7Auxillary tables

(iii) 12 Auxiliary tables (iv) 5 Auxiliary tables

253. Which of the following tables can be added without any instruction to add number from it in DDC?

(i) Table-7 (ii) Table-2

(iii) Table-1 (iv) Table-8

254. "Knowledge Organisation", is a journal which was earlier published under the title:

(i) Journal of Information Organisation.

(ii) Library Journal

(iii) Bulletin of Information Management

(iv) International classification

255. Out of five fundamental categories, which one is easier to identify in a title?

(i) Energy (ii) Levels

(iii) Time (iv) Class Number

256. "Niti-Niti principle" is used to identify:

(i) Personality (ii) Matter

(iii) Space (iv) Energy

257. Broad system of Ordering (BSO) is an initiative of:
   (i) IFLA (ii) UNESCO
   (iii) UNISIST (iv) FID

258. Colon was the only connecting symbol in colon classification upto:
   (i) 6th Ed. (ii) 2nd Ed.
   (iii) 1st Ed. (iv) 3rd Ed.

259. The type of notation used in colon classification is:
   (i) Pure Roman
   (ii) Mixed Notation
   (iii) Indo-Arabic Numerals
   (iv) None of these

260. Delivery of Books and Newspapers (Public) Library Act (India) was passed in:
   (i) 1948 (ii) 1954
   (iii) 1956 (iv) 1903

261. "Term Card" is associated with
   (i) Pre-coordinate Indexing system
   (ii) Post-Coordinate Indexing System
   (iii) Development of Classification Schemes
   (iv) Cataloguing of Rare-documents

262. What term is used in colon classification for "INDEX"
   (i) Bibliography (ii) Not used at all
   (iii) Dictionary (iv) Concordance

263. Seymor Lubetzky is related with

(i) Classification Scheme
(ii) Bibliometric Laws
(iii) Sampling Techniques
(iv) Cataloguing codes

264. First edition of colon classification was published in:
(i) 1933 (ii) 1934
(iii) 1930 (iv) 1928

Answer Sheet

1. (iv)	2. (iii)	3. (iv)	4. (i)
5. (iii)	6. (i)	7. (ii)	8. (i)
9. (iii)	10. (i)	11. (iv)	12. (iii)
13. (iii)	14. (i)	15. (iii)	16. (iv)
17. (iii)	18. (iv)	19. (ii)	20. (ii)
21. (ii)	22. (i)	23. (iii)	24. (i)
25. (i)	26. (ii)	27. (iii)	28. (ii)
29. (i)	30. (iii)	31. (iv)	32. (i)
33. (ii)	34. (I)	35. (I)	36. (iv)
37. (i)	38. (ii)	39. (i)	40. (iv)
41. (ii)	42. (iv)	43. (iv)	44. (ii)
45. (iii)	46. (ii)	47. (iv)	48. (i)
49. (iv)	50. (i)	51. (I)	52. (iv)
53. (ii)	54. (iv)	55. (iv)	56. (iv)
57. (i)	58. (i)	59. (iv)	60. (iii)

61. (i)	62. (i)	63. (ii)	64. (iv)
65. (ii)	66. (i)	67. (iii)	68. (i)
69. (iv)	70. (i)	71. (i)	72. (i)
73. (ii)	74. (i)	75. (iii)	76. (iv)
77. (ii)	78. (iii)	79. (ii)	80. (iii)
81. (iv)	82. (iii)	83. (iii)	84. (ii)
85. (iii)	86. (i)	87. (iii)	88. (iii)
89. (i)	90. (iii)	91. (i)	92. (iv)
93. (ii)	94. (i)	95. (iv)	96. (iv)
97. (ii)	98. (i)	99. (iv)	100. (iii)
101. (iii)	102. (iv)	103. (iii)	104. (i)
105. (iii)	106. (iv)	107. (iii)	108. (iv)
109. (iii)	110. (iv)	111. (iii)	112. (i)
113. (iii)	114. (iii)	115. (iii)	116. (i)
117. (iii)	118. (i)	119. (ii)	120. (iv)
121. (ii)	122. (iii)	123. (i)	124. (i)
125. (iii)	126. (iii)	127. (iv)	128. (iv)
129. (iv)	130. (iv)	131. (i)	132. (iv)
133. (i)	134. (ii)	135. (iii)	136. (iv)
137. (i)	138. (iii)	139. (ii)	140. (I)
141. (ii)	142. (iv)	143. (ii)	144. (iv)
145. (ii)	146. (iii)	147. (ii)	148. (ii)

149. (iii)	150. (ii)	151. (ii)	152. (iv)
153. (iv)	154. (iii)	155. (i)	156. (iii)
157. (iv)	158. (iv)	159. (iii)	160. (iii)
161. (iv)	162. (iii)	163. (ii)	164. (iv)
165. (i)	166. (ii)	167. (iii)	168. (ii)
169. (ii)	170. (iii)	171. (i)	172. (iv)
173. (ii)	174. (iv)	175. (i)	176. (iv)
177. (iii)	178. (ii)	179. (iii)	180. (ii)
181. (i)	182. (ii)	183. (ii)	184. (i)
185. (iii)	186. (ii)	187. (iv)	188. (iii)
189. (iii)	190. (ii)	191. (iii)	192. (iv)
193. (iv)	194. (ii)	195. (iv)	196. (i)
197. (iv)	198. (i)	199. (ii)	200. (iv)
201. (iii)	202. (ii)	203. (iv)	204. (iv)
205. (iii)	206. (iv)	207. (i)	208. (I)
209. (iii)	210. (iv)	211. (ii)	212. (i)
213. (ii)	214. (iii)	215. (iv)	216. (ii)
217. (ii)	218. (ii)	219. (i)	220. (iii)
221. (iv)	222. (i)	223. (i)	224. (iii)
225. (iv)	226. (i)	227. (iv)	228. (iii)
229. (ii)	230. (iii)	231. (ii)	232. (iii)
233. (ii)	234. (iii)	235. (i)	236. (iii)

237. (iv)	238. (i)	239. (ii)	240. (iv)
241. (i)	242. (iii)	243. (iv)	244. (ii)
245. (iv)	246. (ii)	247. (iv)	248. (iii)
249. (ii)	250. (iii)	251. (iv)	252. (ii)
253. (iii)	254. (iv)	255. (iii)	256. (i)
257. (iii)	258. (ii)	259. (ii)	260. (iii)
261. (ii)	262. (iv)	263. (iv)	264. (i)

Unit-V

Library & Information Management

1. Management by objectives (MB) was introduced by:
   (i) Henri Fayol (ii) Peter Drucker
   (iii) Abraham Maslow (iv) Herberk Simon.

2. TQM stands for:
   (i) Total Quality management
   (ii) Time & Quality Management
   (iii) Total Quantity Movement
   (iv) None of these

3. What are the steps involved in MBO?
   (i) Finding the objectives
   (ii) Setting the objectives
   (iii) Controlling and reporting the status of the objectives
   (iv) All of the above

4. Cost Accounting is being done :
   (i) To estimate the financial requirement of next year.
   (ii) To have an idea of past performance.
   (iii) To have an idea of cost involved in providing a service
   (iv) To keep a check on proper use of accounts.

5. "Time-Rate method" is used in:
   (i) Job-Analysis
   (ii) Job-Evaluation
   (iii) Wage-determination
   (iv) Staff-promotion

6. Who is associated with Leadership Grid formation?
   (i) Rensis Likert (ii) Robert R. Blake
   (iii) Kurt Lewin (iv) All of the above

7. Noise in the process of communication is:
   (i) Any message which is additional to main manage.
   (ii) Any hindrance in the communication process
   (iii) Any thing which receiver does not want to listen.
   (iv) It changes with the situation

8. Path-Goal theory is related to :
   (i) Management styles
   (ii) Organisation structures
   (iii) Theory of Leadership
   (iv) None of these

9. Which studies showed that "worker's actions are influenced by the group".
   (i) Studies of Taylor
   (ii) Studies of Elton Mayo
   (iii) Studies of Luther Gullick
   (iv) Studies of Mary Follett

10. Self-Actualizing theory was propounded by:
   (i) Abraham Maslow (ii) Peter Drucker

(iii) Douglas McGregor (iv) Henri Fayol

11. Which analysis shows that cost of providing a service is greater than or less than the value of service.
    (i) Cost-effectiveness analysis
    (ii) Cost-benefit analysis
    (iii) Theory X and Theory Y
    (iv) None of these

12. Which process examines one's productivity with other institutions of same kind?
    (i) Benchmarking
    (ii) Cost-benefit analysis
    (iii) MBD
    (iv) TQM

13. The full-for of PERT is:
    (i) Political, Engineering, reform tools.
    (ii) Planning employee's review techniques
    (iii) Program Evaluation and Review Techniques
    (iv) Performance evaluation and Reporting techniques

14. In McClelland's theory, which need is drive to succeed:
    (i) Need for power
    (ii) Need for affiliation
    (iii) Need for achievement
    (iv) None of these

15. The Thematic Apperception Test (TAT) was conducted by:

(i) Abraham Maslow (ii) Elton Mayo
(iii) Herbert Simon (iv) McClelland

16. Who gives the best expectancy theory of motivation?
(i) B.F. Skinner (ii) McClelland
(iii) Elton Mayo (iv) Victor Vroom

17. Which stud is considered pioneer in showing the importance of the human begins in organizations?
(i) Manto Carlo techniques
(ii) Peter & Drucker studies
(iii) Hawthorne Studies
(iv) Abraham Maslow studies

18. McGregor's Theory X and Theory Y was developed in:
(i) 1901 (ii) 1950
(iii) 1952 (iv) 1960

19. Theory X and Theory Y which one presents positive picture of human beings in an organisation?
(i) Tehroy X (ii) Theory Y
(iii) Both of these (iv) None of these

20. Theory of hierarchy of need sis given by:
(i) AbrahanMaslow (ii) Elton Mayo
(iii) Peter Drvcker (iv) Henri Fayol

21. Who has written "The Wealth of Nations"?
(i) Taylor (ii) Maslow
(iii) Adan Smith (iv) Lancaster

22. What type of organizations are not found on the

organization chart?
(i) Formal organizations
(ii) Informal organizations
(iii) Government organizations
(iv) Non-Government organization

23. In an organization chart, Authority flows:
(i) Top downwards (ii) Bottom Upwards
(iii) Both ways (iv) None of these

24. Grapevine is a type of :
(i) Oral communication
(ii) Formal communication
(iii) Informal communication
(iv) Is a type of fruit

25. Another term for PERT is :
(i) PRT (ii) PEST
(iii) CPM (iv) None of these

26. Which theory supports that "Leaders are born, not made".
(i) Trait approach theories
(ii) Ohio state studies
(iii) Behavioral approach theories
(iv) University of Iowa studies

27. McClelland's need theory gives ____ major categories of human need?
(i) Four (ii) Five
(iii) Three (iv) Two

28. Sold lines in an organization charts shows :
(i) Authority (ii) Staff

(iii) Authority & staff (iv) None of these

29. Monte Carlo techniques are related to :
    (i) Self-Actualizing theory
    (ii) Theory X and Theory Y
    (iii) Decision theory
    (iv) General Systems theory

30. The term Scientific Management was coined in :
    (i) 1876 (ii) 1901
    (iii) 1910 (iv) 1976

31. What does the term Esprit de Corps means:
    (i) Order moves from top to bottom
    (ii) Order moves from bottom to top
    (iii) Is related to communication in horizontal direction.
    (iv) Feeling to move towards a positive cause

32. Another name of "Estimate of income & expenditure":
    (i) Annual Report
    (ii) Budget
    (iii) Committee's report
    (iv) Balance Sheet

33. Which one of the budgeting technique takes past performance as zero?
    (i) Programme budgeting
    (ii) Planning budgeting
    (iii) Line budgeting
    (iv) Zero-based budgeting

34. The standard size of Accession Register is:
    (i) 15" x 15" (ii) 16" x 11"
    (iii) 10" x 16" (iv) 16" x 13"

35. Which one of the following is prepared at the end of a year?
    (i) Accession Register (ii) Annual Report
    (iii) Budget (iv) None of these

36. Statistics of Library resource covers, collection, Finance and
    (i) Furniture (ii) Equipments
    (iii) Staff (iv) All the above

37. What type of construction is now prepared in library buildings?
    (i) Fixed construction
    (ii) Modular construction
    (iii) Concrete construction
    (iv) None of the above

38. PODSCORB is related to :
    (i) Library cataloguing.
    (ii) Information Retrieval
    (iii) Library Administration
    (iv) Indexing rules

39. Which one of the following is more closely related to "Scientific Management"?
    (i) Henri Fayol
    (ii) Luther Gulick
    (iii) Frederick W. Taylor
    (iv) Derek Austin

40. Peter Drucker is associated with:
    (i) Management by Objective (MBO)
    (ii) Scientific Management
    (iii) Development of PRECIS
    (iv) Revision of AACR-1

41. "Three Card System" used in periodical section is devised by:
    (i) Dr. S.R. Ranganathan
    (ii) Derek Austin
    (iii) W.C. Berwick Sayers
    (iv) Antonio Panizzi

42. Which one of the following is not part of "Three Card System"?
    (i) Check Card
    (ii) Classified Index Card
    (iii) Unit Card
    (iv) Register Card

43. Intelligence Tests were suggested by:
    (i) Alfred Binot (ii) H.P. Luhn
    (iii) Mayo (iv) R.N. Anthony

44. Which one of the following charging system is named after the place where it was devised?
    (i) Dickman Book Charging System
    (ii) Gaylord Charging System
    (iii) Scotch Tape Tabs system
    (iv) Newark Charging System

45. A minimum amount per head of population is fixed in :

(i) Proportional Method
(ii) Per capital method
(iii) Browne Method
(iv) Methods of details

46. Incunabula is a term denoting:
(i) Government Archives
(ii) Archives of eminent persons
(iii) Books printed before 1500
(iv) Collection of manuscripts

47. Which one of the following is not part of "Scientific Management"?
(i) Job Analysis
(ii) Incentive wage system
(iii) Division of Labour
(iv) None of these

48. The UGC's Library Committee (1957) suggested that _____ of the total expenditure of a University Library should be spent on books, periodicals, and the _____ should be spent on staff.
(i) 50% ; 50% (ii) 30% ; 70%
(iii) 70% ' 30% (iv) 45% ; 55%

49. Line of formal authority moves from:
(i) Top to bottom
(ii) Bottom to top
(iii) Top to Horizontal
(iv) Top to bottom and Horizontal both

50. Which one of the following is generally last step in financial administration?

(i) Auditing (ii) Budgeting

(iii) Wage distribution (iv) Budget Estimation

51. Who is related with "Theory Y and Theory Y"?
    (i) Douglas McGregor
    (ii) Abraham Maslow
    (iii) Peter Drucker
    (iv) Herbett Simon

52. Who propounded the Goal-Setting theory?
    (i) McGregor (ii) McClelland
    (iii) B.F. Skinner (iv) Edwin Locke

53. What type of performance appraisal methods are most commonly used?
    (i) Essay methods
    (ii) Rating Scales
    (iii) Forced distribution methods
    (iv) Graphic rating scale

54. "Essay methods" are used in an organisation:
    (i) In place of interview methods
    (ii) In writing complaints about staff
    (iii) In writing complaints of staff
    (iv) As employee appraised

55. Information is key to the process of :
    (i) Policy formation
    (ii) Decision making
    (iii) Budget making
    (iv) Annual Report Writing

56. The standard size of Accession Register is :
    (i) 16 x 13 inch (ii) 12 x 15 inch

(iii) 15 x 16 inch (iv) None of there

57. Which one is part of communication process:
    (i) Source (ii) Channel
    (iii) Receiver (iv) All of the above

58. Which one is not part of Job Analysis?
    (i) To find out what is to be done.
    (ii) To find the best method of doing it.
    (iii) To fix the money value for it.
    (iv) To determine qualification needed by a worker to do it.

Answer Sheet

1. (ii)	2. (I)	3. (iv)	4. (iii)
5. (iii)	6. (ii)	7. (ii)	8. (iii)
9. (ii)	10. (i)	11. (ii)	12. (i)
13. (iii)	14. (iii)	15. (iv)	16. (iv)
17. (iii)	18. (ii)	19. (Ii)	20. (i)
21. (iii)	22. (ii)	23. (i)	24. (iii)
25. (iii)	26. (i)	27. (iii)	28. (i)
29. (iii)	30. (iii)	31. (iv)	32. (ii)
33. (iv)	34. (iv)	35. (ii)	36. (iv)
37. (ii)	38. (iii)	39. (iii)	40. (i)
41. (i)	42. (iii)	43. (i)	44. (iv)
45. (ii)	46. (iii)	47. (iv)	48. (i)
49. (i)	50. (i)	51. (i)	52. (iv)
53. (iv)	54. (iv)	55. (ii)	56. (i)
57. (iv)	58. (iii)		

Unit-VI

Computer & Information Technology

1. AND, OR and NOT are types of operations:
   (i) Simple alphabetic terms
   (ii) Qualifying operators of PRECIS
   (iii) Computer operators
   (iv) Boolean operators

2. Which computer generation is now-a-days in use?
   (i) Fifth Generation
   (ii) Fourth Generation
   (iii) Fourth Super Generation
   (iv) Fifth Plus Generation

3. ISDS stands for:
   (i) International Subscribers Dialing Service
   (ii) International Standard Document delivery services
   (iii) International Standard Digital Services
   (iv) International Serials Data System

4. Which part of computer can be used as both Input/Output devices:
   (i) Joystick (ii) Monitor
   (iii) Printer (iv) Keyboard

5. Charles Babbage, developed a machine in 1812, known as:

(i) Difference Engine (ii) ENITC

(iii) EDSAC (iv) IBM computes

6. Which open of the following is not a "Search Engines"?

(i) Altavista (ii) Web Crawler

(iii) Excite (iv) Netscape Navigator

7. "COM" stands for:

(i) Computer operated Machines

(ii) Computer Output on microforms

(iii) Computer output in Machine Readable form

(iv) Computer output on Microfilm

8. "SANJAY", a library software was developed by:

(i) INSDOC (ii) DESIDOC

(iii) NISSAT (iv) UNESCO

9. "MAITRAYEE", a library software was developed by:

(i) Informatics (India) Ltd.

(ii) DESIDOC

(iii) UNESCO

(iv) CMC Ltd.

10. Which one of the following network topology is most commonly used?

(i) Star Network (ii) Tree Network

(iii) Meshed Network (iv) Ring Network

11. What type of network topology was recommended in INFLIBNET?

(i) Star topology

(ii) Distributed topology

(iii) Mesh topology

(iv) Hierarchical topology

12. To convert analog signals into digital and vice-versa, the___ is used:

(i) Hub (ii) Switch

(iii) Modem (iv) Server

13. Which one of the following provides fast communication link?

(i) Paired cables (ii) Microwave radio

(iii) Coaxial cables (iv) Optical fibres

14. Packet switching is used in:

(i) Library software development

(ii) Library database development

(iii) Making communication between two computers

(iv) All of the above

15. ISDN stands for :

(i) International Subscriber Dialling Network

(ii) Integrated Services Digital Network

(iii) Integrated Subscribers Digital Network

(iv) None of these

16. Microwave signals are sent using:

(i) More than 12 GHz frequency

(ii) Less than 2 GHz frequency

(iii) 2-12 GHz frequency

(iv) 12-24 GHZ frequency

17. In Satellite Communication, a satellite is placed at ____ miles above earth.

(i) 22300 (ii) 11,000

(iii) 20,600 (iv) 11,600

18. Which one of seven-layer is first layer in data transport?
    (i) Layer 1 (ii) Layer 7
    (iii) Layer 3 (iv) Layer 6

19. Which one of the following Layers form the core of most network protocols?
    (i) Layer 1 (ii) Layer 7
    (iii) Layer 3-4 (iv) Layer 4-7

20. DSL stands for :
    (i) Direct Service Locator
    (ii) Digital Subscriber Line
    (iii) Digital Service Line
    (iv) None of these

21. Open Systems Interconnection (OSI) is related to:
    (i) Database design
    (ii) Operating software
    (iii) Communication protocols
    (iv) Indexing rules

22. Which one of the following is not a layer described by OSI in communication process?
    (i) Data Link Layer (ii) Network Layer
    (iii) Sender Layer (iv) Physical Layer

23. In how many layers, OSI divides the communication process?
    (i) 7 (ii) 8
    (iii) 9 (iv) 6

24. Layer 1-3 deals with:
    (i) Data transmission
    (ii) End-to-end communication
    (iii) Data receiving
    (iv) None of these

25. Telephone is an example of :
    (i) Uni-directional communication
    (ii) Bi-directional communication
    (iii) Both (i) & (ii)
    (iv) None of these

26. Information travel speed is measured in
    (i) Giga Hertz (ii) kbps
    (iii) bps (iv) Km/sec.

27. CAT-5 is a kind of:
    (i) Unshielded twisted wring
    (ii) Optical fibre
    (iii) shielded twisted wiring
    (iv) Electrical wiring

28. If in a network, cable ends are not joined then it is:
    (i) Bus topology (ii) Mesh topology
    (iii) Star topology (iv) Ring topology

29. The term "Bandwidth" represents:
    (i) Max. capacity it can transmit
    (ii) Both of these
    (iii) Max speed with which it
    (iv) None of these

30. Which one of the following protocol is used in transferring file over Internet?
(i) FTP (ii) SMTP
(iii) POP (iv) TCP/IP

31. URL stands for:
(i) Uniform Research Leader
(ii) Uniform Resource Locator
(iii) Universal Resource Locator
(iv) Universal Resource Location

32. A URL is stored in _____ field of MARC
(i) 800 (ii) 830
(iii) 856 (iv) 956

33. Apache is a kind of
(i) Open Source software
(ii) Licensed software
(iii) Both of these
(iv) None of these

34. Who is the originator of ETHERNET?
(i) Robert Metcalfe (ii) Lancaster
(iii) Richard Metcalfe (iv) Vickerey

35. Linux is an example of:
(i) Application software
(ii) System software
(iii) Library software
(iv) All of the above

36. Which one of the following is mulk-user operating system ?

(i) MS-DOS (ii) Windows-98

(iii) COBOL (iv) UNIX

37. Which part of computer system is known as 'Brain of Computer"?
(i) Motherboard
(ii) CPU
(iii) Memory
(iv) Hard Disk Drive (HDD)

38. MEDLARS is a service provided by:
(i) National Library of Medicine, USA
(ii) National Medical Library, New Delhi
(iii) National Science Library, New Delhi
(iv) Library of Congress, USA

39 ENVIS network is located at :
(i) Department of Electronics, Govt. of India
(ii) Department of Electrical Engineering, University of Delhi.
(iii) Department of Environment, Govt. of India
(iv) Department of Environment, Govt. of U.K.

40 SIRNET stands for:
(i) Sri Lankan Information Network
(ii) Scientific Information Network
(iii) Subjective Information Network
(iv) Scientific and Industrial Research Network

41 DEVINSA is information network of:
(i) South Asia (ii) South Africa
(iii) South Australia (iv) South Avenue

42. DOI is web resources is equivalent to _____ of book.
    (i) ISBN
    (ii) Statement of responsibility
    (iii) Call Number
    (iv) Accession Number

43 National Aeronautical Laboratory (NAL) is having:
    (i) NISSAT Sectoral Centre for compact Disc
    (ii) NISSAT sectoral centre for chemicals
    (iii) NISSAT sectoral centre for Crystalles rely
    (iv) NISSAT sectoral centre for Advanced Ceramics.

44 DESIDOC Library is considered as :
    (i) National Science Library
    (ii) National Defence Library
    (iii) India Input Centre for INIS
    (iv) UNESCO supported Public Library

45. Which one of the following Biblometric laws deals with frequency of occurrence of words in a text?
    (i) Lotka's Law (ii) Ziff's Law
    (iii) Brandford's Law (iv) Pritchard's Law

46 The Spiral of Scientific Method involves the following steps (in correct sequence)
    (i) Zenith, Ascendant, Nadir, Descendant, Zenith
    (ii) Descendant, Zenith, Ascendant, Nadir, Descendant
    (iii) Ascendant, Nadir, Zenith, Descendant, Ascendant

(iv) nadir, Ascendant, Zenith, Descendant, Nadir

47. OCLC Inc. stands for:
   (i) Online College Library Centre
   (ii) Ohio College Library Centre
   (iii) Online Catalogue of London Colleges
   (iv) Ohio College Libraries Catalogue

48. 'Law of Scattering' is propovided by:
   (i) Lancaster (ii) Bradford
   (iii) Zipf (iv) Garfield

49. The term "Biblometrics" was first used by:
   (i) Dr. S.R. Ranganathan
   (ii) FW Lancaster
   (iii) Alan Pritchard
   (iv) Allen Kent

50. "MEDLARS" is a kind of :
   (i) Information System
   (ii) Abstracting Journal of INSL
   (iii) Information Generator
   (iv) Indexing system in Mumbai

51. VIKRAM, a data network is established by:
   (i) Department of Electronics
   (ii) Department of Telecommunications
   (iii) Informatics (India) Ltd.
   (iv) Ministry of Defence

52. Ahmedabad, City of India is having:
   (i) Headquarters of ILA
   (ii) Headquarters of NISSAT

(iii) Information Centre of ISRO

(iv) Information & Library Network (INFLIBNET)

53. "NISCAIR" an orgnaisation of CSIR is created by

(i) An Independent body under the UNESCO Grant.

(ii) Combining INSDOC and NISCOM

(iii) Combining INSDOC and NISTAD of CSIR

(iv) Bifurcating UGC

54. The full-form of DELNET is

(i) Detriot Library Network

(ii) Delhi Library Network

(iii) DELL Computer Library Network

(iv) Developing Library Network

55. CDS/ISIS Software was developed by:

(i) National Science Library, New Delhi

(ii) Libsys Corporation, India

(iii) British Museum

(iv) UNESCO

56. UNISIST stands for:

(i) UNESCO System for Science & Technology

(ii) Union of Scientific Information System & Technology

(iii) United Nations Information System for Science & Technology

(iv) United Nations Intellectual Services for Science & Technology

57. UNISIST is a programme of :

(i) IFLA (ii) UNESCO

(iii) ASLIB (iv) Indian Government

58. SENDOC is located at
    (i) Kolkata (ii) Pune
    (iii) Hyderabad (iv) Nagpur

59. Which one of the following is commercial network?
    (i) VIKRAM (ii) ERNET
    (iii) INDONET (iv) NICNET

60. INFLIBNET was made operational under:
    (i) Seventh Plan (ii) Eighth Plan
    (iii) Sixth Plan (iv) Fifth Plan

61. CALIBNET is the network of:
    (i) Chennai City (ii) Chicago City
    (iii) Calcutta City (iv) Kanpur City

62. Which one of the following is an international information system?
    (i) NISSAT (ii) DEVSIS
    (iii) INTELSAT (iv) INSAT

63. The term "Automation" was first time used by :
    (i) Lancaster (ii) H.P. Luhn
    (iii) Pascal (iv) D.S. Harder

64. Which one of the following is National Centre for India in INIS?
    (i) BARC, Trombay
    (ii) NISCAIR, New Delhi
    (iii) DESIDOC, New Delhi
    (iv) ISRO, Bangalore

65. "METRON" is a:
    (i) International Library Network
    (ii) IACE Publication

(iii) International Information System in Medicine

(iv) Current Awareness Journal Published by INSPEC

66. Which one of the following system acts as ”World Science Information System”?

(i) ISORID (ii) OCLC

(iii) PGI (iv) UNISIST

67. NISSAT network consist of :

(i) Sectoral System

(ii) Regional system

(iii) Specialized services

(iv) All of the above

68. CDS/ISIS (Microversion) is developed by:

(i) UGC (ii) UNESCO

(iii) UNISIST (iv) UNO

69. “ENVIS” stands for:

(i) Electronic Information System

(ii) Engineering Information System

(iii) Environmental Information System

(iv) None of the above

70. NICNET has its regional centres at :

(i) Pune (ii) Bhubaneswar

(iii) Hyderabad (iv) All of the above

71. UNISIST is served by information from India through:

(i) NISCAIR (ii) National Library

(iii) NISTADS (iv) NISSAT

72. National Information Centre for Machine Tool and Production Technology (NICMAP) is located at :
   (i) New Delhi (ii) Bangalore
   (iii) Mysore (iv) Chennai

73. Which NISSAT, sectoral centre is located at Lucknow:
   (i) NICFOS (ii) NICRYS
   (iii) NICDAP (iv) NICMAP

74. What is full form of BHEL?
   (i) Birla Heavy Equipment Limited
   (ii) Bharat Heavy Electricals Limited
   (iii) Bangalore Hardware Engineering Lab.
   (iv) Bombay Heavy Engineering Limited

75. MEDLINE is a service provided by:
   (i) National Medical Library (USA)
   (ii) National Library of Medicine (India)
   (iii) Library of Congress (USA)
   (iv) National Science Library (India)

76. National Information Centre for Crystallography (NICRYS) is located at:
   (i) Chennai (ii) Mysore
   (iii) Pune (iv) Bangalore

77. INPADOC is an :
   (i) International Patent Documentation Centre
   (ii) Indian Patient Documentation Centre
   (iii) Internet Protocol Documentation Centre
   (iv) International Periodical Delivery Centre

78. International Standards Information Network (ISONET) is:
    (i) Geneva (ii) Hague
    (iii) Chicago (iv) Paris

79. Which one of the following is member of POPIN in India?
    (i) Ministry of Health
    (ii) National Medical Library
    (iii) NIHFW
    (iv) National Science Library

80. Which city out of following does not have NISSAT regional centre?
    (i) Lucknow (ii) New Delhi
    (iii) Chennai (iv) Pune

81. PIPIN network is related to :
    (i) Poverty Information
    (ii) Physics Information
    (iii) Political Science Information
    (iv) Population Information

82. BRS is a search service of:
    (i) NASA (ii) NML
    (iii) INIS (iv) CIA

83. DIALOG is a software originally developed for :
    (i) NML (ii) NSL
    (iii) NASA (iv) CIA

84. MEDLARS used ____ software in their searching.
    (i) Orbit (ii) Dialog
    (iii) BRS Search (iv) Linux

85. Dublic core is used to :
    (i) Exchange Information
    (ii) Catalog web resources
    (iii) Transport data over optical fibres
    (iv) None of these

86. Dublin Core (DC) consist of :
    (i) 15 elements (ii) 10 elements
    (iii) 25 elements (iv) 08 elements

87. Which one of the following is Indian input centre for ISDS:
    (i) Central Secretariat Library
    (ii) IARI
    (iii) National Library
    (iv) NISCAIR

88. National Information Centre for Food Science (NICFOS) is located at:
    (i) Chennai (ii) Pune
    (iii) Mysore (iv) New Delhi

89. INSDOC was set up in :
    (i) 1952 (ii) 1947
    (iii) 1950 (iv) 1945

90. JANET stands for :
    (i) Japan Network
    (ii) Jordan Network
    (iii) Joint Academic Network
    (iv) Joint Administrative Network

91. "Granthalaya" is a library software developed by:

(i) DESIDOC (ii) DRTC
(iii) INPADOC (iv) NISCAIR

92. Z39.50 is a standard for:
(i) Communication formats
(ii) Search and retrieve services
(iii) Cataloging web resources
(iv) Library Management Services

93. First Search is a service of:
(i) DIALOG (ii) OCLC
(iii) DRBIT (iv) LISA

94. UNICODC is used in exchange of :
(i) Sensitive Information
(ii) Bilingual Information
(iii) Spanish Information only
(iv) None of these

95. PGI stands for :
(i) Programme on General Information.
(ii) Programme general de information
(iii) Printed Guidebook of Information
(iv) None of the above

96. In BLCMP, the letter 'B' denotes.
(i) British (ii) Bombay
(iii) Birmingham (iv) Banaras

97. Food Science and Technology Abstracts (FSTA) is published from:
(i) India (ii) USA
(iii) Paris (iv) U.K.

98. NISSAT's sectoral information centes for Bibliometric studies is located at :
    (i) Nagpur (ii) Chennai
    (iii) Ahmedabad (iv) Bangalore

99. "TRAILS" is a system for :
    (i) Document organization in INSDOC
    (ii) Document organization in SENDOC
    (iii) Internet Surfing Software
    (iv) Indexing techniques

100. "MINISAS" is developed by:
    (i) UNESCO (ii) NISSAT, India
    (iii) Libsys, India (iv) IDRC, Canada

Answers

1. (iv)	2. (ii)	3. (iv)	4. (ii)
5. (i)	6. (iv)	7. (iv)	8. (ii)
9. (iv)	10. (i)	11. (iv)	12. (iii)
13. (iv)	14. (iii)	15. (ii)	16. (iii)
17. (i)	18. (ii)	19. (iii)	20. (ii)
21. (iii)	22. (iii)	23. (i)	24. (i)
25. (ii)	26. (iii)	27. (iii)	28. (i)
29. (i)	30. (i)	31. (ii)	32. (iii)
33. (i)	34. (i)	35. (ii)	36. (iv)
37. (ii)	38. (i)	39. (iii)	40. (iv)
41. (i)	42. (i)	43. (i)	44. (ii)
45. (ii)	46. (iv)	47. (i)	48. (ii)
49. (iii)	50. (i)	51. (ii)	52. (iv)

53. (ii)	54. (iv)	55. (iv)	56. (iii)
57. (ii)	58. (iii)	59. (iii)	60. (ii)
61. (iii)	62. (ii)	63. (iv)	64. (i)
65. (iv)	66. (iv)	67. (iv)	68. (ii)
69. (iii)	70. (iv)	71. (iv)	72. (ii)
73. (iv)	74. (ii)	75. (i)	76. (i)
77. (i)	78. (i)	79. (iii)	80. (i)
81. (iv)	82. (iv)	83. (iii)	84. (i)
85. (ii)	86. (i)	87. (iv)	88. (iii)
89. (i)	90. (iii)	91. (iv)	92. (ii)
93. (ii)	94. (ii)	95. (iii)	96. (iii)
97. (iv)	98. (iii)	99. (ii)	100. (iv)

Unit-VII

Research Methodology

1. The "Chi Square test" is related to :
   (i) Data Selection
   (ii) Data Analysis
   (iii) Hypothesis formation
   (iv) Conclusion drawing

2. Random Sampling is of following ____ types:
   (i) Four (ii) Three
   (iii) Five (iv) Six

3. A sampling technique where, population is divided into similar groups and then sample is made:
   (i) Cluster sampling
   (ii) Systematic sampling
   (iii) Simple Random Sampling
   (iv) Stratified Random sampling

4. Systematic sampling is where :
   (i) Population is first divided into similar groups, then sampling is done.
   (ii) Selection of each "n^{th}" number of a list is done.
   (iii) Selection of data is done by lottery method.
   (iv) None of the above.

5. "Ascendent" is spiral of scientific method sis related to :

(i) Accumulation of facts

(ii) Accumulation of empirical laws

(iii) Accumulation of fundamental laws

(iv) Accumulation of deduced laws

6. Spiral of scientific method divides spiral into:

(i) Four quadrants (ii) Six quadrants

(iii) Two quadrants (iv) Three quadrants

7. "Co-citaton" stands for:

(i) Number of times a pair of document is commonly cited

(ii) Process of listing he references

(iii) Analysis of references given at he end of document

(iv) List of all kinds of publication of a person.

8. "Half-Life" value of a literature shows:

(i) productivity of scientific literature

(ii) Unusable state of scientific literature

(iii) Obsolescence of scientific literature

(iv) None of the above

9. JCR stands for:

(i) Journal of Chemical Research

(ii) Journal Classification Report

(iii) Journal Cited Report

(iv) Journal Citation Report

10. "Quadrant 2" is also termed as :

(i) Deductive phase (ii) Empirical phase

(iii) Verification phase (iv) Hypothesing phase

11. Formulation of hypothesis is related to :
    (i) Point of Nadir
    (ii) Point of Zenith
    (iii) Point of Ascendent
    (iv) Point of Descendent

12. Refinement of Bradford's law of scattering was done by:
    (i) Alfred Lotka (ii) Zipf
    (iii) Lancaster (iv) Vickerey

13. Which one of the following step is not involved in systematic research?
    (i) Identification and definition of the problem.
    (ii) Formulation of hypothesis
    (iii) Formulation of conclusions
    (iv) None of the above

14. Which one of the following is not a main research methods?
    (i) Experimental (ii) Field Study
    (iii) Descriptive (iv) Historical

15. S.C. Bradford analysed the literature of Geophysics and ______ to give law of cattering?
    (i) Geochemistry (ii) Lubrication
    (iii) Laser Technology (iv) Biochemistry

16. If two consecutive references appear on a same page, then second reference will be written as :
    (i) Op cit (ii) Ibid
    (iii) The work cited (iv) Same as above

17. If a sample of 20 were to be taken out of 200

students of 8th standard, then this type of sampling will be :

(i) Area sampling (ii) Stratified sampling

(iii) Cluster sampling (iv) Systematic sampling

18. Which one of the following is a research tool of data collection?

(i) Random Sampling (ii) Roget's Thesaurus

(iii) Questionnaires (iv) The Chi Square test

19. The science which deals with quantitatively analysis of recorded knowledge:

(i) Documentation

(ii) Informatics

(iii) Statistical bibliography

(iv) Bibliometrics

20. Bibliographical coupling is related to :

(i) Bibliometric studies

(ii) Bibliography compilation

(iii) Modes of subject formation

(iv) Vocabulary control

21. The law which describes the productivity of authors with in the subject field is:

(i) Lotka's Law (ii) Bradford's Law

(iii) Zipf's Law (iv) Pritchard's Law

22. Which one of the following is related to "Bibliographic coupling".

(i) Alfred Lotka (ii) S.C. Bradford

(iii) Kessler (iv) Ranganathan

23. Which one of the term was coined by Ranganathan?

(i) Bibliometrics (ii) Scientometrics
(iii) Librametry (iv) Photometry

24. "Cole and Eales" are related to the publication of:
    (i) Journal of Documentation
    (ii) Statistical Bibliography
    (iii) Prolegonema of Library Science
    (iv) The title of comparative anatomy

25. "Law of least Resistance" was proposed by:
    (i) Zipf (ii) Bradford
    (iii) Lotka (iv) Pritchard

26. What does the term "Net Exporters" mean:
    (i) Information transfer to other place
    (ii) Subjects that are cited more than they cite
    (iii) Subjects that cites more than they cite
    (iv) None of the above

27. The type of research where the tested observation results and empirical methods are further proven is known as :
    (i) Observation research
    (ii) Empirical research
    (iii) Priori research
    (iv) Pragmatic research

28. If a subject cites more than they are cited, then it is called:
    (i) Nodes (ii) Net importers
    (iii) Links (iv) Net exporters

29. "Score Carde" is a kind of tool for:
    (i) Data Analysis (ii) Data Collection
    (iii) Data Generation (iv) Sampling

30. The number of reference per paper is known as:
    (i) Citation need
    (ii) Simple References
    (iii) Referencing Intensity
    (iv) Citation half-life

31. What is the bottom point of four cardinal points in spiral of scientific method called?
    (i) Ascendant (ii) Nadir
    (iii) Zenith (iv) Descendant

Answers

1. (iv)	2. (ii)	3. (iv)	4. (ii)
5. (i)	6. (iv)	7. (iv)	8. (ii)
9. (iv)	10. (i)	11. (iv)	12. (iii)
13. (iv)	14. (iii)	15. (ii)	16. (iii)
17. (i)	18. (ii)	19. (iii)	20. (ii)
21. (iii)	22. (iii)	23. (i)	24. (i)
25. (ii)	26. (iii)	27. (iii)	28. (i)
29. (i)	30. (i)	31. (ii)	

Unit-VIII

True or False

1. Fifth law makes it duty of state Authority to provide library service.
   (i) True (ii) False

2. IATLIS is a library association of technical staff.
   (i) True (ii) False

3. UNESCO has issued the manifesto for public libraries.
   (i) True (ii) False

4. Andrew Carnegie was an information scientist.
   (i) True (ii) False

5. Nalanda Library is of recent origin.
   (i) True (ii) False

6. National Library of India is located at Chennai.
   (i) True (ii) False

7. Saraswati Mahal Manuscripts Library is located at Tanjore.
   (i) True (ii) False

8. DESIDOC serves as a focal point in India for UNISIST.
   (i) True (ii) False

9. Mudalair commission was setup in 1952.

(i) True (ii) False

10. NICTAS is located at Ahmedabad.
(i) True (ii) False

11. Andhra Pradesh is the first state to implement library legislation.
(i) True (ii) False

12. INIS is a program of Library of Congress.
(i) True (ii) False

13. Kothari Commission was set up to look after the working of Public Libraries.
(i) True (ii) False

14. DESIDOC is a focal point in India for all IMS activities.
(i) True (ii) False

15. ILA was established in 1947.
(i) True (ii) False

16. OCLC stands for Online computer library centre.
(i) True (ii) False

17. ALA is a library association of Africa.
(i) True (ii) False

18. NUCCSI is published by NSL.
(i) True (ii) False

19. IFLA is located at Dublin.
(i) True (ii) False

20. Walford's Guide to Reference material is published from United Kingdom.

(i) True (ii) False

21. Atomindex is published by INIS.
    (i) True (ii) False

22. DESIDOC is working under DRDO.
    (i) True (ii) False

23. Survey of India is located at New Delhi.
    (i) True (ii) False

24. John Macfarlane was the fist librarian of Imperial Library at Kolkatta.
    (i) True (ii) False

25. Imperial Library was opened to the public in 1908.
    (i) True (ii) False

26. Delivery of Books (Public Libraries) Act was passed in1952.
    (i) True (ii) False

27. Maharaja Sayajirao-I of Baroda was the pioneer of Library movement in the state.
    (i) True (ii) False

28. Headquarters of RRRLF is located at New Delhi.
    (i) True (ii) False

29. K.P. Singh Advisory Committee for Libraries was set up under second five year plan.
    (i) True (ii) False

30. University of Bombay was established in 1946.
    (i) True (ii) False

31. Laws of Interpretation is a kind of law at sub-

division level.

(i) True (ii) False

32. Open Access is supported by first law of library science.

(i) True (ii) False

33. Harward University Library was the first library of America.

(i) True (ii) False

34. The first library was set up in America in 1853.

(i) True (ii) False

35. Press and Registration of Books Act in India was passed in 1867.

(i) True (ii) False

36. In 1958, Delivery of Books Act was amended to include Newspapers in it.

(i) True (ii) False

37. Andhra Pradesh was the first state to made provision of state Librarian in its Act.

(i) True (ii) False

38. Maharasthra Public Library Act was passed in 1967.

(i) True (ii) False

39. Gujarat Public Libraries Act was passed in 1998.

(i) True (ii) False

40. India Copyright Act was by British Government in the year 1914.

(i) True (ii) False

41. Annual Report of a library can be a means of public relation's promotion.
    (i) True (ii) False

42. Organisation of lectures is a type of extension service of library.
    (i) True (ii) False

43. Mobile Library Service is a part of Library outreach progamme.
    (i) True (ii) False

44. Association for Information Management was earlier known as ASLIB.
    (i) True (ii) False

45. The frequency of ILA Bulletin is monthly.
    (i) True (ii) False

46. The first Library school was started by Dr.S.R. Ranganathan in India.
    (i) True (ii) False

47. FID/CCC is responsible was revision of DDC.
    (i) True (ii) False

48. Universal Bibliographic Control (UBC) is a pogamme of IFA.
    (i) True (ii) False

49. Copyright Bulletin is a publication of UNESCO.
    (i) True (ii) False

50. Indian Dissertation Abstract is a publication of NISCAIR.
    (i) True (ii) False

51. Code of Ethics of ALA was adopted in 1938.
(i) True (ii) False

52. GOC stands for Good Officer Committee.
(i) True (ii) False

53. JOCLAI is a association of India.
(i) True (ii) False

54. Decachotomy is division into two.
(i) True (ii) False

55. Dr. S.R. Ranganathan in 1944 identified Dissection as a mode of formation of subjects.
(i) True (ii) False

56. Deductive Logic is formed due to the process of denudation.
(i) True (ii) False

57. Biochemistry has evolved to the effect of fusion.
(i) True (ii) False

58. Kant's system of philosophical classification was dichotomy system.
(i) True (ii) False

59. APUPA pattern was given by F W Lancaster.
(i) True (ii) False

60. Library of Congress classification is a purely remunerative clasificaiton scheme.
(i) True (ii) False

61. Latest edition of colon classification in 8th ed.
(i) True (ii) False

62. In DDC, 600 stands for History.
    (i) True (ii) False

63. Indo-Arabic Numerals are totally used in UDC.
    (i) True (ii) False

64. The Plus Sign (+) is used in UDC for representing a series of corrective class numbers.
    (i) True (ii) False

65. A number is square brackets ([ ]) in DDC denotes an important class number.
    (i) True (ii) False

66. Letter (x) in color classification stands for economics.
    (i) True (ii) False

67. Author Catalogue is a kind of physical catalogues.
    (i) True (ii) False

68. Unit card system was introduced in Library of Congress in 1901.
    (i) True (ii) False

69. Anthony Panizzi is associated with British Museum cataloging rules.
    (i) True (ii) False

70. AA code stands for American Association Code.
    (i) True (ii) False

71. ISBD (2) divides bibliographic data into seven areas.
    (i) True (ii) False

72. Five laws of library science was published in 1931.
(i) True (ii) False

73. Reference books are read from first to last page
(i) True (ii) False

74. NUCSSI is published by DESIDOC
(i) True (ii) False

75. Current Biography is published from New York.
(i) True (ii) False

76. Union Catalogue is a secondary source of information:
(i) True (ii) False

77. INB is published from Central Secretariat Library.
(i) True (ii) False

78. The principle of SCI is derived from Shepard's Citations:
(i) True (ii) False

79. LISA is published by Bowker Saur.
(i) True (ii) False

80. A gazetteer is a source for information about geographical area
(i) True (ii) False

81. The objectives of a library catalogue were defined by C.A. cutter in 1876.
(i) True (ii) False

82. The frequency of chemical abstracts is monthly.
(i) True (ii) False

83. Library catalogues serve the inventory functions only.
    (i) True (ii) False

84. Ohio College library center was established in 1876.
    (i) True (ii) False

85. Bibliography shows the place of books on shelves.
    (i) True (ii) False

86. In AACR-2 entry for author John P. McGregor will as McGregor (JP)
    (i) True (ii) False

87. Book Index entry is prepared in AACR-I
    (i) True (ii) False

88. Theory of library catalogue first mentioned chain procedure in 1938.
    (i) True (ii) False

89. Sought links are those links by which user search information.
    (i) True (ii) False

90. POPSI was developed by an American
    (i) True (ii) False

91. Indian Library Association was established in 1933.
    (i) True (ii) False

92. Calvin Mooers is related to pre-coodinate indexing.
    (i) True (ii) False

93. In Colon classification term concordance is used in place of Index.
    (i) True (ii) False

94. Index Medicus is published by National Library of Medicine.
    (i) True (ii) False

95. BIOSIS stands for Business Information Service.
    (i) True (ii) False

96. First edition of AACR-I was published in 1876.
    (i) True (ii) False

97. In CCC any information taken from outside source in to placed in square brackets.
    (i) True (ii) False

98. Documentation Research and Training Centre is located at Bangalore.
    (i) True (ii) False

99. Paul Otlet's name is associated with Indexing.
    (i) True (ii) False

100. Trinity of library consists of Books, students and furniture.
    (i) True (ii) False

Answer

1. False	2. False	3. True	4. False
5. False	6. False	7. True	8. False
9. True	10. True	11. False	12. False
13. False	14. False	15. False	16. False

17. False	18. True	19. False	20. True
21. True	22. True	23. False	24. True
25. False	26. False	27. False	28. False
29. True	30. False	31. False	32. False
33. True	34. False	35. True	36. True
37. False	38. True	39. False	40. True
41. True	42. True	43. True	44. True
45. False	46. False	47. False	48. False
49. True	50. False	51. True	52. True
53. True	54. False	55. False	56. True
57. True	58. True	59. False	60. True
61. False	62. False	63. False	64. False
65. False	66. True	67. False	68. True
69. True	70. False	71. True	72. True
73. False	74. False	75. True	76. False
77. False	78. True	79. True	80. True
81. True	82. False	83. False	84. False
85. False	86. False	87. False	88. True
89. True	90. False	91. True	92. False
93. True	94. True	95. True	96. False
97. False	98. True	99. False	100. False

Unit-IX

Fill in the Blanks

1. W.A. Border was related to the Library movement in ______.

2. Advisory Committee for Libraries was appointed under the Chairmanship of__________.

3. Lord ______ was associated with the enactment of Imperial Library Act.

4. National Science Library of India is located at.

5. Headquarter of ALA is situated at ___________

6. International Conference on cataloguing was held in ____ at _______

7. Mobile Library is a kind of _______________

8. Library Orientation is a part of __________________

9. Centralized Acquisition of Periodicals (CAP) in India is provided by _______.

10. Current Awareness Service is provided in ________ of demand.

11. World of Learning is a _______ source of information.

12. Unpublished seminar reports are termed as _____________

13. "Dissertation Abstracts International" is published b ________

14. "Indian National Bibliography" was started in ________

15. "Indian Books in Print" is published by ________________

16. "Index Translation" is a publication of ________.

17. The "Index" equivalent in color classification. __________

18. Two types of reference service are _____ and Long Range reference service.

19. Biotechnology is formed due to _____ of two fields.

20. Table 5 of DDC is for _______________

21. DDC is a _______ classification scheme.

22. 22nd edition of DDC was published in ______.

23. Law of Parsimony is one of the _______ formulated by Dr.S.R.Ranganathan.

24. A person who designs a classification scheme, is known as ______

25. "Ayurveda" in colon Classification is _________ .

26. In Colon Classification, Mother Country is represented by_________

27. Personality, Mother are types of _______ given by Dr. S.R. Ranganathan.

28. The latest edition of color classification is __________.

29. Wall picture principle is used in __________.

30. A characteristic divides a Universe in atleast _____ groups.

31. Canon of Terminology is a canon for ____________

32. The letter 'W' in colon classification stands for ____________

33. The headquarter of CRG is located at ____________

34. Charles Ammi Cutter is associated with the laws of ___________

35. The last of Canon introduced in Cataloguing is ____________

36. In chain procedure, connecting symbols represent_____________

37. Cross Reference Index Entry (CRIE) is prepared under ___________

38. A________ is used in AACR-II to join two parallel titles.

39. The standard size of card catalogue is ____________

40. In AACR-2, connecting symbol between name of publisher and yea of publication is __________.

41. POPSI is a product of ________.

42. Earlier BB was using ________ for deriving subject headings.

43. H.P. Luhn's name is associated _____ type of Indexing.

44. UNITERM INDEX is a type of ______ indexing technique.

45. Originator of Citation Index is __________.

46. Thesaurus is a kind of _________ devices.

47. The publisher of Sear's list of subject headings is __________

48. The concept of coordinate indexing is given by _________________

49. The term Information was in _______.

50. The full-form of UF is _________.

51. Differential Piece work was given by ___________

52. Hawthorn Studies were conducted by __________

53. Esprit de Corps stands for _______________

54. Order goes from _____ to ______.

55. Flow of Information is from _____ to ________

56. A budgeting techniques where the previous year details are not taken into account is __________.

57. Nina F.Browne devised the ________________

58. Dr S.R.Ranganathan was ________________ of Banaras Hindu University

59. Central reference Library publishes ________.

60. SANJAY, library software was developed by ___________

61. UNIX is a kind of _________.

62. In Computer technology "ADA" is a kind of _______

63. The headquarter of OCLC is located at __________

64. According to C.W. Hanson, informations can be of ________types.

65. Patents are ________ source of information.

66. Conversation with colleagues is a ________ source of publication.

67. The term "Communication" is derived from Latin word.________

68. According to S. Parasarthi, the whole communication process comprise of ________ elements.

69. A IIT Library is a kind of ____________________.

70. Translation service is a solution to ________ barrier in communication.

71. The "Information retrieval" was coined by ________________

72. MEDLINE is a service of ____________________

73. Index of a document consist of descriptor and its __________

74. The Index of DDC is a __________ index.

75. The publisher of Library Literature is ________________

76. Chain Indexing was first used in _________ Library.

77. DEAP is associated with ____________________.

78. The role operator (6) in PRECIS stands for

____

79. The display format of PRECIS consists of ________ part.
80. W.E. Batter was associated with ________ indexing.
81. FORTRAN is a type of ________ language.
82. The latest computer generation is ________.
83. COMENDEX is a indexing service in ________
84. Headquarter of DELNET is located at ________
85. "Liberation" is a kind of ________
86. CDS/ISIS is developed by ________.
87. Maitryi is developed by ________.
88. Optical Coincidence system is also known as ________
89. The frequency of SCI is ________.
90. Institute of Scientific Information is located at ________
91. Vatican code is related to ________ .
92. IN AACR-II, there are ________ levels of description.
93. AACR-II, Part-II is related to ________.
94. Chapter-4, AACR-II is related to ________ cataloguing.
95. The code of cataloguing of the Smithsonian Institute is associated with ________.

96. There were _________ libraries behind the preparation of AACR-2.

97. Encyclopedia Britannia is divided into _________ parts

98. Collier's Encyclopedia is published from ________.

99. The second law of library science is ____.

100. In 1979 _____ Public Library Act was passed.

Answer Sheet

1 Baroda

2 Shri S.K. Sinha

3 Lord Curzon

4 NISCAIR, New Delhi

5 Chicago

6 1961, Paris

7 Extension service

8 User Education

9 NISCAIR, New Delhi.

10 Anticipation

11 Secondary

12 Grey Literature

13 University Microfilms, USA

14 1957

15 Indian Bibliographies Bureau

16 UNESCO

17 Concordance

18 Short Range Ref. Service

19 Fusion

20 Racial, Ethnic, Notional

21 Almost Enumerative

22 2003

23 Basic Laws

24 Classification

25 System

26 One (1)

27 Fundamental Category

28 7th

29 Facet Sequence

30 Two

31 Political Science

32 London

33 London

34 Dictionary Catalogue

35 Canon of Recall value

36 False Link

37 Classified Catalogue Code

38 Slash

39 12.5cm by 7.5cm

40 Semi Color

41 DRTC, Bangalore

42 Chain producer

43 KWIC

44 Post Coordinate

45 Shepard

46 Vocabulary Control

47 H.W. Wilson

48 First used

49 USA

50 Use for

51 F.W.Taylor

52 Elton Mayo

53 Morale

54 Top, Bottom

55 Bottom, Top

56 Zero based budgeting

57 Browne Charging/discharging system

58 University Librarian

59 INB

60 DESIDOC

61 Operating System

62 Programming Language

63 Dublin

64 Source (two)

65 Primary

66 Informal

67 Communicate

68 Five

69 Special

70 Foreign Language

71 Calvin Mooers

72 National Medical Library, USA

73 Location

74 Relative

75 H.W. Wilson

76 Madras University

77 POPSI

78 Target/Form

79 Three

80 Post coordinate

81 High Level

82 4th

83 Engineering

84 New Delhi

85 Library Software

86 UNESCO

87 CMC Ltd.

88 Peek-a-boo system

89 Quarterly

90 Philadelphia

91 Cataloguing

92 Three

93 Determination and establishment of access points

94 Manuscript

95 Charles C. Jewelt

96 Five

97 Three

98 New York

99 Every reader His/Her Book

100 West Bengal

Jaikrishnadas Ayurveda Series
484

A COMPREHENSIVE GUIDE TO MARMA THERAPY

VITAL POINTS

BHARTI MURLIDHAR TAHIL

CHAUKHAMBHA ORIENTALIA
A House of Oriental, Antiquarian and Ayurvedic Books
Varanasi • Bangalore

Vital Points (A Comprehensive Guide To Marma Therapy)
by Bharti Murlidhar Tahil

ISBN : 978-93-89091-45-8
Pages : 20 + 260

First Edition : 2025

Publishers :
CHAUKHAMBHA ORIENTALIA
K. 37/109, Gopal Mandir Lane, Golghar, Maidagin
Varanasi, Uttar Pradesh - 221001
Phone: 0542-2333476, 2334356, +91 7379884433
E-mail: co@chaukhambha.com • info.covns@gmail.com

Branch :
1st floor, No. 2602, 26th Main, 38th Cross, Jayanagar 9th Block,
Bangalore, Karnataka - 560041
Phone: +91 8105740600
E-mail: info.coktk@gmail.com

www.chaukhambha.com

Disclaimer: The author disclaims any liability, for injury or risk whatsoever, which incurred as a consequence of any direct or indirect use of information given in this book. All information is for educational purposes only, and is not intended as a substitute for the medical advice of physicians.

Printed by: Charu Printers, Golghar, Varanasi